THE SMART GUIDE TO

Wedding Weekend Events

How to Plan Fabulous Cocktail Parties, Sporting Events, and Other Fun Activities During Your Wedding Weekend's Downtime

By Sharon Naylor

Author of *The Smart Guide to Bachelorette Parties*

The Smart Guide To Wedding Weekend Events

Published by
Smart Guide Publications, Inc.
2517 Deer Creek Drive
Norman, OK 73071
www.smartguidepublications.com

For information, address: Smart Guide Publications, Inc. 2517 Deer Creek Drive, Norman, OK 73071

SMART GUIDE and Design are registered trademarks licensed to Smart Guide Publications, Inc.

International Standard Book Number: 978-0-9785341-2-7

Library of Congress Catalog Card Number2011924540

11 12 13 14 15   10 9 8 7 6 5 4 3 2 1

Printed in *the United States of America*

Cover design: Lorna Llewellyn

Copy Editor: Ruth Strother

Back cover design: Joel Friedlander, Eric Gelb, Deon Seifert

Back cover copy: Eric Gelb, Deon Seifert

Illustrations: Lorna Llewellyn

Sharon Naylor Photograph: Rich Penrose

V.P./Business Manager: Cathy Barker

For my mom, Joanne, and in memory of my father, Andrew~
Thank you for a delightful wedding weekend filled with the best of everything a girl could ever want—loving family, friends from near and far, laughter, dancing, great food, and memories that last a lifetime.

ACKNOWLEDGMENTS

Thanks and cheers to my amazing agent Meredith Hays for her bright guidance of my newest projects, her unfailing sense of humor, and her friendship.

I'd also love to thank the team at Smart Guides for inviting me into their family and welcoming me to stay around for a while.

And, finally, my gratitude to my illustrious colleagues in the wedding industry. I'm so lucky to work in a field filled with such admirable, supportive, charming, and noncompetitive luminaries. It's a dream come true to count myself among you all.

And, as always, thanks and love to my husband, Joe, who co-created our own wedding weekend filled with fabulous cocktail parties, downtime with our bridal party, and romantic, loving surprises for me. You were the best part of it all.

TABLE OF CONTENTS

NOTE FROM THE AUTHOR

You're going to have such a fantastic and fun-filled wedding weekend, and I wish I could be there to enjoy it all with you!

With your fabulous plans for outings, cocktail parties, adventure sports, and classy cultural events, you give such a great gift to your wedding guests! They've put a lot into attending your wedding, no matter how far they travel, and it's delightful when they get to look forward to additional social events and laid-back gatherings that allow them to enjoy quality time with relatives and friends they don't see often enough.

This wedding, then, becomes legendary, the best one anyone's been to in years (perhaps ever), all because of the variety and creativity of your planned wedding weekend celebrations, competitions, kids' events, and more.

Thank you for allowing me to help you along in your planning, and I would love to hear all about the weekend events you've planned. You may even appear in the next edition of this book! So visit me at www.sharonnaylor.net or join my Facebook Fan Page, message me on Twitter, or meet me at a booksigning near you.

All the very best,
Sharon Naylor

INTRODUCTION

A fabulous, unforgettable, dream wedding weekend is filled with wonderful celebrations, and we're not just talking about the ceremony and reception. While those events are the gorgeous, meaningful center of any wedding weekend, what's become the new must is planning a lineup of posh parties, day trips, sporting competitions, gourmet get-togethers, and so many more exciting experiences that give the bride and groom what they really want: more time to spend with their friends and family.

In today's global society, which has friends and family members living all over the state, the country, and the world, the occasion of a wedding now creates a thrilling reunion, bringing loved ones together for the first time in ages. Brides and grooms want so much more than the five minutes they'd get to spend with their far-flung friends at their reception.

"We wish we planned lots of social events during our wedding weekend! At our wedding, we barely got any time at all to spend with our friends, since we were being pulled away by relatives or called to the dance floor or guided away by our photographer for more portraits. The reception flew by, and when it was all over, we were upset that guests who had traveled so far to share this day with us barely got to spend five minutes with us; and we didn't get to hang out with them, either. If we could do it again, we'd plan a dozen wedding weekend parties, a girls' a day out, a round of golf for the guys, so many fun things to share with everyone!"—Elise and Mitchell, newlyweds

Elise and Mitchell aren't alone. So many brides and grooms say that the one disappointment of their wedding celebration was not getting enough quality time with their favorite people, so the hot, new trend of planning wedding weekend events is here!

If guests are going to travel to attend a wedding, it's now a must to give them lots of fun activities to look forward to. If parents aren't going to be planning as much of the wedding as they used to in years past, it's now a must for them to plan their own wedding weekend parties for the couple, or just for their friends to share time with them.

There's no end to the perks of filling a wedding weekend with lots of fabulous, fun activities, and you have in your hands the guide that's going to help you choose the perfect event theme and style so that you can plan a get-together that everyone will love and talk about for years as a highlight of the wedding weekend. You might be the bride or groom, you might be a parent, a sister, a friend, a bridesmaid—anyone can plan a wonderful wedding weekend event that gives guests the time of their lives! And many friends and relatives who do plan wedding weekend parties and get-togethers are making their hosted events their wedding gift to the bride and groom. That's how much the wedding couples loves them.

Here are just some of the most popular wedding weekend events, taking place during the days prior and after the wedding, being planned for and by the bride and groom:

> ➤ Welcome cocktail parties
>
> ➤ Barbecues
>
> ➤ Pool parties and trips to the beach
>
> ➤ Softball tournaments
>
> ➤ Rounds of golf at a private golf club
>
> ➤ A celebrity-inspired spa party by the pool
>
> ➤ Winery tours
>
> ➤ Shopping sprees in the big city

Of course, included in this list are the traditional rehearsal dinner and morning-after breakfasts that have long been a part of the wedding weekend, as well as the fairly new trend of the post-reception after-party. This book will help you get a head start on these expected events and so many others into new and improved, creatively inspired celebrations that everyone will be raving (and posting on Facebook and Tweeting) about!

With this book, you have the equivalent of a celebrity event planner helping you plan, design, personalize, and pull together any type of wedding weekend event in style and on a budget. For each party theme, you'll find dozens of planning tips, creative inspirations, money-smart ideas, and more. Just look for these boxed features:

> ➤ **Steal My Party Idea**: Real-life party planners tell you about the brilliant things they planned, and encourage you to do the same.
>
> ➤ **Watch Out!**: A quality party planner will steer you away from making expensive party-wrecking mistakes.
>
> ➤ **Etiquette Friendly**: Since it's still a wedding weekend, there are some etiquette rules you'll need to follow.
>
> ➤ **Money Mastery:** These tips will help you save tons of money on your event plans.
>
> ➤ **Shop Here!**: These websites share some of the best website offerings out there.

As you read through this book, take notes, flag pages, combine themes and styles to personalize your own custom event that the bride, groom, and every guest will love. Use the worksheets and resources in the back of the book to keep yourself organized and plan efficiently and smartly, and hang on to this book for the next wedding weekend when you can be the host of a smash hit soiree that the next bride and groom will love you for.

Ready to plan an amazing wedding weekend event? Let's get started right now.

PART ONE

The Basics

CHAPTER 1

 # Planning Multiple Events

In This Chapter

➤ Varying the events for different groups

➤ Comfortable scheduling for weekend events

➤ Following planning etiquette

The average wedding weekend—from the arrival of the first guests a day or two before the big day to the departure of guests a day or two after the wedding itself—lasts at least four days. And in some situations, such as destination weddings, holiday weekend weddings, and cultural wedding celebrations, the festivities may stretch across five or more days. So that provides plenty of time for multiple wedding weekend events.

In this chapter, you'll figure out how many separate events can be planned so that guests have plenty of activities to choose from, and so that everyone (including the very busy bride, groom, and their families) gets plenty of mingling time with family and friends. During today's wedding weekend, the average number of planned events is three, but you can go beyond that. Some groups plan three per day for those various groups and cliques of family and friends to enjoy. For instance, the day after the wedding might begin with a morning-after breakfast for the out-of-town guests, a barbecue and pool party for guests who are staying in town an extra day, a thank-you cocktail party hosted by the bride and groom for their bridal party, and an evening event hosted by the parents for their own circle of friends and family. That's four right there.

Planning for Different Groups

Don't be limited by the belief that every social event has to be all-inclusive, that you can only plan parties and outings that all of the guests would like to attend. You can plan some all-inclusive events but also schedule specialty events to be enjoyed by smaller groups of friends or family or both.

Brides and grooms of the past often report just one disappointment with their wedding weekends: they felt spread too thin at the wedding, and they didn't get enough time with long-distance friends they haven't seen in years. Table-hopping and greeting guests at the wedding gave them only a few minutes with those friends, and then they were whisked away to take photos or asked to dance or were interrupted by something else. The new class of wedding weekend events, particularly a cocktail party planned just for the bride's and groom's circle of friends, allows them hours of downtime and very satisfying quality time with people they don't get to see often enough.

Parents too enjoy having the option to plan their own social events for just their own closest friends and family they don't get to see often enough. And there's another perk to parents planning their own private events: in this era of the bride and groom taking ownership of the wedding plans, parents who want to share in the planning—and may be pushy with their ideas—get to be the boss of their own parties. That gives them creative control of *an* event, not *the* event. Brides and grooms love that, and suggest to pushy parents that they plan their own smaller guest list parties and bask in the glow of their guests' raves about their home, menu, décor, and so on.

Money Mastery

If you're thinking about planning a wedding weekend event, you're likely concerned that it would cost a fortune to invite and feed all of the people invited to the wedding, or even just the big list of out-of-towners who are coming in for the big day. The advent of smaller, private group parties cuts down your expenses tremendously. Your budget will stretch further for fifteen guests as opposed to fifty.

Here are just some of the types of groups that might have their own events:

➤ Immediate family

➤ Immediate family plus out-of-town family

➤ The bridal party and their guests

➤ The bride's and groom's local and long-distance friends

➤ The friends and family of the bride's parents

➤ The friends and family of the groom's parents

➤ Guests with small children (invited to child-oriented parties or a family movie)

Should You Plan a Singles Event?

You might have expected to see single guests on the list above, but it's quickly become a don't to plan an event just for singles. During a weekend filled with dating, and engaged and married couples, some singles don't want to be herded into a matchmaking event, feeling like they're being set up. "At one wedding weekend party, the bride and groom didn't tell me that this was a single-mingle party, and while I get that they were just being nice and trying to help, it made me feel even more self-conscious about not being in a relationship. When friends are getting married, I feel pretty left behind," says Mina, a friend of the bride.

Mina's take on a singles-only party represents what some singles feel, not all. Some singles might be thrilled to get a speed-dating event filled with the groom's hot cousins and friends. But bear in mind that singles can do fantastic mingling and flirting at events that include paired-up couples. In fact, happily partnered or married friends make the best wingmen or wingwomen, finessing introductions and singing the praises (subtly) of their single friends. For this reason, plus the possible sensitivity of some singles, more couples are planning happy hours and other events to include paired and single friends, rather than special events just for singles.

Tailoring Party Themes and Styles to Groups of Guests

In this book, you're about to explore many different themes and styles of parties, from classic cocktail parties to spa parties, outings to museums and festivals, golf outings, theater performances, at-home movie nights, and more. Think about the group you're planning for, and decide which type of event would be the most enjoyable for them. For instance, a gathering of your girlfriends from near and far might call for a pampering spa party enjoyed in your home, catered, with expert manicurists there to treat everyone. Guests with kids in tow will appreciate your planned kid-friendly swim party. Parents' friends, grandparents, and the golden-ager set might far more enjoy an at-home dinner party than a group outing to a sports bar where your friends can catch a playoff game, eat wings and fries, and down pitchers of beer (or perhaps the grandparents would *love* that!)

Watch Out!

Before you make plans—and book a party bus—for a trip to a big city, or print up invitations to a big cultural festival that demands lots of walking during the summer months, or any other outdoor, exertion-filled event, check with the bride and groom (or with in-the-know relatives) to be sure such an event would be doable for all of the guests. If there are elderly, disabled, very pregnant, or injured guests on crutches, that kind of event is something they might choose to skip, to the disappointment of the bride and groom.

Another thing to keep in mind is that guests may see this wedding weekend as a time to relax, step away from their too-hectic lives, get away from it all, and just chill. Those who may be spending a day traveling from afar to get to the wedding town may especially love a more laid-back schedule. So, again, talk to the bride and groom about their wished-for activity levels, and perhaps the ideal get-together is just an afternoon spent by the hotel's pool with a casual gathering afterward. No packed itinerary and scheduled musts, departure times, and the like.

Money too is a big factor in the kind of event you plan. Will you be able to afford tickets to a play or museum for fifty guests? Will you expect the guests to pay for their own tickets? Would the family be offended if you ask them to do so? It's something to keep in mind when you're deciding on the type of event to plan.

Ideal Weekend Scheduling

You'll explore your options for timing social events in the next chapter, but it's important to keep in mind that many parts of the wedding weekend may be already booked for the bride and groom, and that they'll likely have meetings and appointments pop up closer to the big day.

You have to look for available pockets of time when your event may take place, and keep your event on the short side. It's not realistic to plan an all-day event during a wedding weekend, but a two- or three-hour get-together in the evening may be a good fit. The bride and groom can then enjoy your casual party after a long day of meetings and other tasks are done.

Brides and grooms say that they love it when friends and family offer to host wedding weekend events, but they feel pressured when too many are planned. They feel pressured to attend, and those days before the wedding are filled with more intense emotions, exhaustion, nerves, and short fuses. Not just their own, but those of their parents and others around them. You may think that a social event is just what they need, but what they might need is an hour or two to themselves to take a bath or go for a solo run. Thus, brides and grooms say that having just a few extra-special events planned for them works best.

Etiquette for Planning Wedding Weekend Events

Whether you plan to host a wedding weekend event or you're the bride or groom, keep the following important etiquette rules in mind:

➤ Always check with the bride and groom before you plan or announce your party so that they can either clear your plan or let you know if there's a conflict, in which case you would need to alter your plans. It's their wedding weekend, after all. Not deferring to the bride and groom makes it seem like you're purposely planning a party during their spotlight time so that you can shine or take advantage of mutual friends' travel plans for the wedding, stealing them away from the bride and groom. That's likely not your intention, but you don't want to be saddled with that impression.

➤ If you're the bride or groom, it's in poor taste to ask friends and family members to throw you a party or host an event. Ideally, the hosts will come to you with their offers to host in your honor. (I know, you're probably horrified by the idea that anyone would do this, but I have heard from some wedding guests who have been stunned at a nervy request like this made by a wedding couple who felt entitled to the best that others could pay for.)

➤ If you're the bride or groom and multiple parties are planned, it's okay for you to event hop to visit as many as possible; it's also okay for you to skip private parties such as your parents' cocktail party for their friends. You'll see those guests at the wedding, and they'll understand that you have a lot going on right now.

➤ Give guests plenty of notice about planned wedding weekend events so that they can make their travel plans accordingly. Some book their airfare months and months in advance, so they'll need to know about the wonderful day-after friends-only party you have on the schedule, one they'd hate to miss.

➤ When you send invitations for your event, be sure to include a URL or link to the location of the party as well as full details about any ticket prices or costs associated with the event in question. It would be terrible for guests to board your party bus and then find out that they have to pay the $20 ticket fee for each member of their family to get into the show, museum, or other attraction. That information needs to be shared up front, so that guests can decide if they'll join you on this particular outing.

➤ It's perfectly okay to invite guests to these events via Evite.com, even if the wedding will be a very formal one.

➤ If a party is set to be a small VIP event, avoid posting anything about it on Facebook or other social media. You don't want uninvited people to feel left out or to contact you to ask if they can come—with a guest. Yes, that's bad etiquette on their part, but you can avoid that diplomacy headache just by keeping any mention of your private party off of your profiles.

➤ Of course, the bride or groom should send a thank-you note and possibly a gift to the hosts of any get-togethers planned in their honor as soon after the event as possible.

 **Finding Time Slots**

In This Chapter

➤ Day-by-day plan

➤ Timing your party

➤ When you have to cancel a party

In this section, you'll fine-tune your party plans to suit the wedding weekend schedule. If the only time that's open for you to host a party is after dinner—by request of the bride and groom—then only certain types and styles of events will work. If only mornings are available, then forget about holding a cocktail party or dinner, obviously.

Here, you'll look at the wedding weekend calendar to see which days and which times are available and a good fit for the type of party or outing you'd like to plan. Some events can be tailored to suit any time of day, such as a morning, afternoon, or evening pool party, so you may find that your desired party plan is possible, but just has to be shifted to a different time of day than you had originally envisioned.

The goal is to offer and host a party that fits the bride and groom's already packed weekend without adding any stress to them. The result is a fabulous get-together that everyone enjoys fully, adding even more joy and togetherness to the couple's most special weekend ever.

Days of the Week

As mentioned earlier in this book, some guests—such as bridal party members—arrive in town a few days before the wedding to be available for last-minute tasks and celebrations. And in the case of many destination weddings, the bride and groom may plan the trip to start several days before their planned ceremony and reception days. So the window of opportunity for a prewedding party when a wedding is scheduled for Saturday may begin on Thursday. Using this time frame as an example, we'll walk through some possible events that you might choose to plan for each day of a wedding weekend.

Thursday

Call this arrival day, and bear in mind that many guests have had a full, exhausting day of travel, perhaps waking up in the wee hours to get to the airport. Since those travelers are most likely to stay in the local hotel where a block of rooms have been booked, the check-in time of the hotel may have determined their travel plans. For instance, a 3 pm check-in is just the start of when they'd be able to settle into the rooms. Some guests arrive ahead of check-in time, and some arrive hours later. To allow all a bit of settling-in time before the activities begin, I advise not planning anything before the evening hours of arrival day.

Watch Out!

"Our original plan was to have a welcome cocktail party going for when our guests were checking in, but that turned into a huge disaster when some guests' flights were delayed, or they stopped off to eat before getting to the hotel and didn't show up until two hours after the check-in time. We wound up stuck at the hotel lounge for four hours, paying for everyone's drinks the whole time, while other guests trickled in. And even then, we missed out on welcoming those who arrived really late."–Kate, bride

The idea of a welcome cocktail party is a great one, but it works better when you schedule it to begin at a later evening time, such as 7 pm or 8 pm. The later timing also removes you from the responsibility of picking up dinner for all of these arriving guests if you don't wish to foot that bill. According to the same etiquette rules of weddings, a party that starts at 5 pm or so tells guests that dinner will be served. Some people may eat their dinner at 7 pm, but the overarching etiquette rule says that from 7 pm onward is not considered to be dinner hour so serving dinner is not required. So you're exempt from that expense, and guests will arrange dinner on their own. Many guests say that they like having the free hours upon arrival to meet up with their close friends or relatives they haven't seen in years, and those small groups are likely to venture off to have dinner together, on their own.

With your arrival-day cocktail party timing set, you can arrange to have guests meet you in the hotel lounge, where you'll pick up the tab for drinks and appetizer platters that everyone can share. To keep your budget under control, make this party only one or two hours long. Set an end time with the bar manager when you prebook this event—and be sure to prebook this event, not just show up with no plan in place, so that the staff can accommodate your budget-saving end time. At 9 pm, say, the check is brought to you, the tab is closed, the official party's over, and then guests are free to stay on, open their own tabs, and continue their evening. You'll find more details about planning a welcome cocktail party in chapter 7, including menu ideas, budget choices for drinks, and more. This section is just about timing.

Another option for arrival day is the party *after* the welcome cocktail party. That would be a get-together at your place, in your hotel suite, or at a nearby restaurant, with just your closest friends on the guest list. It could be just four of you or a group of six or eight—not a large group, not a party, just a relaxing get-together. You'll find plenty of entertaining ideas for this type of private party in chapters 7 and 9.

Friday

Most guests, and perhaps even the bridal party, will be arriving on this common day before the wedding, and the same arrival-party plans may be set for this day as well.

Since this is the day before the big day, it's to be expected that the bride and groom have the events schedule set. The rehearsal will be planned for a certain time and place, and the rehearsal dinner will also be planned for a certain time and place. In an upcoming chapter, you'll explore both traditional and new, trendy ideas for the rehearsal dinner, so look ahead for planning details, personalization tips, and budget smarts for this event, and keep in mind that it's not always the case that all out-of-town guests will be invited to the rehearsal dinner. In past years, many bridal couples felt it was the thing to do, but when a large number of out-of-town guests are invited, an all-inclusive rehearsal dinner winds up being the same scale and cost as the wedding itself! So in that rehearsal dinner chapter, you'll find ideas for a separate event just for those out-of-town guests who are not in the wedding party.

Watch Out!

Don't plan an elaborate, expensive party for the late afternoon to evening hours the day after the wedding unless you've already confirmed with friends and family that they will be able to attend. You don't want to invest time and money in a social event that gets wrecked when no one's going to be in town long enough to attend. And keep in mind that some guests who originally plan to stay the next day may find themselves departing sooner than planned due to hangovers, date drama, babysitter snafus, and general anxiety about workloads and obligations awaiting them at home. Impending bad weather may also force quicker departures than expected.

The pocket of time after the rehearsal dinner, which may end at 8 pm, could be a great time to plan one of those private guest list get-togethers with long-distance friends or with the bridal party. Read on for more ideas in that realm.

And, of course, if a Friday night wedding is planned, that event is the entirety of Friday's schedule.

Saturday

If this is wedding day, the expected lineup of events is the wedding morning breakfast—see chapter 10 for ideas!—the salon trip (perhaps featuring a champagne breakfast for the bride and her bridesmaids and moms), the wedding and reception, and perhaps a spontaneous or planned and themed after-party for the couple's and the parents' guest lists.

Sunday

We're calling this the day after the wedding, and it starts with a morning-after breakfast that may be planned for the couple, immediate family, bridal party, and out-of-town guests. Again, t chapter 10 has full planning details. We're just looking at an events lineup right now.

After breakfast, guests who plan to stay on until the evening hours or to the next day may be invited to any of the wedding weekend events listed here in this book. You might throw a casual barbecue, a beach party, a softball tournament followed by a cookout, tours, or any number of other special social events detailed in this book. If you have a whole day available with late-departing guests, this is where the newest trends in wedding weekend events have really exploded, with the wedding weekend taking on the excitement of a family-and-friend reunion.

Look at afternoon events primarily, since most guests will depart at about 3 pm to allow travel time and adapting to their at-home routines and chores.

Time of Day

Look at the available time slots to help you configure the type and style of event you'll host. This chart of start times will help you find your way:

> ➤ Early morning events (like biking outings and hikes): 7 am to 9 am

> ➤ Morning events (like breakfasts and tennis matches): 9 am to 11 am

> ➤ Early afternoon events (like lunches and tours): noon to 2 pm

> ➤ Late afternoon events (like festivals and sporting events): 2 pm to 4 pm

➤ Early evening events (like cocktail parties and dinners): 5 pm to 7 pm

➤ Evening events (like dinners and theater performances): 7 pm to 9 pm

➤ Late night events (like clubbing and comedy club outings): 9 pm onward

These are the traditional start times for different types of events, and you might find that your wished-for event can fit into two or more possible time slots. For instance, a pool party might start at noon, or it might start at 3 pm to avoid peak UV hours. I provide this list just as a guide to help you create your event plans according to open time slots and the best convenience times for guests.

Always be sure to print on your itinerary an end time for the event so that guests can decide if the timing works for them and doesn't conflict with preparing for a nighttime event or scheduling a get-together with other guests.

Money Mastery

Another factor to keep in mind is that some times of day will provide for a more affordable outing. An early hour dinner— such as 5 pm—at a restaurant could get you a lower per-person cost than a dinner event that starts at 7 pm. Talk to the restaurant manager to ask about early bird pricing and special prix fixe menus that take place between 5 pm and 7 pm and will save you a bundle of money. The same goes for specialty tours. A professional tour company may charge your group a lot less for a 10 am event than a tour taking place during their busier hours in the afternoon. When it comes to group activities, ask about the best-priced timing.

Cancelling the Party

For any number of reasons, whether it's a schedule conflict with something the bride and groom have planned—even at the last minute—or guests arriving late due to inclement weather, you might need to cancel your event. If that is the case, your first course of action is e-mailing or texting all guests who have RSVP'd to your party to let them know of the change in plans. Ask them to send you confirmation that they've received your message so that you know all guests are in the know about the change in plans.

Your next course of action is figuring out what to do with any food you've acquired for the event. Talk to the bride and groom to find out if they or another wedding weekend event host would like you to bring your party fare to their place. In the case of last-minute cancellations, you'll likely have shopped for and prepped some dishes, so it's a smart decision to offer your generous supply to anyone who'd like to supplement their buffet.

Etiquette Friendly

If you do offer your canceled party fare to another host for her spread, it's not in good etiquette to ask her to pay you for it. If she offers, you can accept if you wish. But most people are concerned with creating a special event for the bride, groom, and guests to truly enjoy, no matter where the party takes place.

CHAPTER 3

Formality Mix

> ## In This Chapter
>
> ➤ Keeping guests comfortable
>
> ➤ The price of entertaining
>
> ➤ Do the right thing

The best wedding weekends feature events in a range of formalities, giving guests the chance to enjoy both dressed-to-the-nines, upscale occasions and more relaxed, informal get-togethers. Brides and grooms say that an array of formalities allows them to enjoy the best of both worlds as well. If, for instance, their budget allows for a less formal wedding such as a casual beach or backyard celebration, they can still look forward to a formal dress-up rehearsal dinner. If the wedding will be formal or ultra-formal, they can look forward to casual parties where they can wear jeans (or bathing suits) in laid-back ease.

In this chapter, you'll explore the benefits of planning events in a range of formalities, looking as well at the budget break that may be achieved through less formal styles of parties and outings.

"We wanted our wedding to stand out as the most formal part of the weekend," says Tasha, a recent bride. "We didn't have the budget to go way over the top for our wedding plans, and we didn't want anyone else's party to outshine our reception. So we planned, and requested from other hosts, only super-informal events around it. Casual food, little to no décor, just iPod music at those parties so that everything we planned for our day would be more impressive and special to us. It worked out perfectly."

Clearly, not outshining the bride and groom's wedding is of the utmost importance. While it is true that some brides and grooms agree to a parent hosting a formal rehearsal dinner—with upscale everything, including lavish décor, caviar, and champagne—when their wedding reception plans are far more reserved, that situation is likely planned in express agreement between the couple and the parents. If you're neither of these two, always consult with the bride and groom about their wished-for formality and party style, even if it is your home and your money involved.

Comfort Issues

Spotlight stealing aside, one of the main reasons to provide some informal events during the wedding weekend is that most guests feel more comfortable when they can dress casually and enjoy comfort foods, as opposed to the which-fork-should-I-use pressures of an ultra-formal event. There's something freeing about dressing down, wearing flats, drinking straight from a beer bottle, and snacking on pigs in a blanket. Guests also enjoy the free-to-roam style of a barbecue or cocktail party as opposed to a formal sit-down dinner.

More relaxed, informal social events facilitate mingling, picture taking, and joking around, providing the perfect balance in a wedding weekend that may include one, two, or perhaps three formal events. So which are the top informal events to blend into the weekend's schedule? Here they are:

➤ Backyard barbecue and pool party

➤ At-home dinner served buffet style

➤ Tours and outings to festivals and cultural events

➤ Movie night, at the theater or at home

➤ Spa and pampering party (It doesn't get more laid-back that that!)

Watch Out!

Brides and grooms don't like surprises. You might think it would delight them if you were to tell them you're planning a casual barbecue, then surprise them with a formal, elegant, tented party with $300 floral arrangements, filet mignon, lobster tails, and Cristal champagne—because they deserve it—such a grand gesture could create a vortex of hurt feelings. Perhaps the couple's parents wish they could afford a grand scale party. They may feel like you're showing them up or showing off your home and entertaining prowess. It may sound ridiculous that your surprise would be taken this way, but emotions are heightened and tensions high during a wedding weekend, and egos may be easily bruised. So make it a rule: clear your true party plans with the bride and groom before you take any steps in planning your event.

You might think that it's the women who enjoy socializing without Spanx and high heels, but men are equally pleased at the chance to avoid wearing a suit, tie, and formal shoes. And not to be forgotten, child guests tend to behave better when they're wearing comfortable clothes as opposed to dresses and tights or suits.

Money Issues

A formal party almost always requires additional expenditures due to a more upscale menu that can include lobster, clams, shrimp, filet mignon, and the like, as well as grand floral centerpieces and additional décor, entertainment, pricy invitations, favors, and other accoutrements. I say *almost always* because it is possible to plan a high-budget informal party, such as a backyard barbecue with a grill menu including bacon-wrapped filet mignon, chicken breasts, stuffed portabello mushrooms, ten different sides, and three different desserts, plus a massive collection of imported beers and wines. You can certainly go high budget at an informal party, but it's a bit more challenging to go low budget at a formal event.

An informal get-together may be catered with budget-friendly platters purchased at Costco or WalMart, or with two-for-one pizzas, which is a strong selling point for those who choose to host informal wedding weekend events.

And, of course, some informal events such as softball games at the park or trips to the beach come with no price tag at all, which might move this type of event to the top of your possibilities list.

Steal My Party Idea

"As a bridesmaid, I was spending over $700 on my dress, shoes, the bridal shower, and other requirements, so I knew I didn't have the budget for a formal event. But I still wanted to host a get-together for the bride and groom and our friends. What I decided on was a movie night at my place, where we watched a DVD that I borrowed from a friend and ate snacks such as chips and salsa, kettlecorn, and mini meatballs. The whole thing cost me $20!"—Lisa, bridesmaid

Etiquette Issues

You never want to outshine any event that the bride and groom has planned, or that has been planned by the parents. Call that etiquette rule number one.

Etiquette rule number two is letting guests know about the styles of wedding weekend events, so that they can pack their clothing, shoes, and accessories properly. For instance, if you tell guests that an event is a trip into the city to tour a museum, you need to tell them that lunch will be at a nearby nice restaurant, and provide the restaurant's URL and a note saying, "The restaurant has a no-jeans policy, so do dress accordingly." People will know from that to wear a skirt or nice pants and a sweater for this particular outing.

If you'll be hosting a pool party or trip to the beach, let guests know to pack bathing suits for the whole family. If a sporting event, such as a softball game, is on the schedule, guests need to know to pack clothes and sports shoes they can play in.

If you'll be hosting host an outing to a nightclub, guests need to know to pack a little black dress or other going-out clothes and shoes. If the hotel brunch is formal enough to have a no-jeans rule, guests need to know. If the rehearsal dinner restaurant requires men to wear jackets and ties, guests need to know. You'll convey these dress codes in the e-mailed or printed invitations that you send to the guests invited to each event. It's considered an etiquette don't to leave dress code information off of any wedding weekend event invitation.

Finally, etiquette rule number three is letting guests know if they will be responsible for paying for any event tickets, cover charges, or other expenses associated with the event. Normally, the host pays all expenses, but if your group always splits the tab at a bar, or if friends have already said they'd love to go to that concert and are happy to pay their own way so that it can happen, always remind them via invitation that some charges will be their responsibility.

CHAPTER 4

Creating Guest Lists

> ## In This Chapter
>
> ➤ Creating a guest list
>
> ➤ Creating a guest list diplomatically
>
> ➤ Avoiding overlap

The big question when it comes to planning wedding weekend events is who gets invited. Hosts not wanting to leave anyone out of a fun wedding weekend get-together become very nervous about the possibility of paying for many more guests than they can easily afford. But as you'll see in this chapter, you don't have to invite all the wedding guests to your party. Besides, it's quite common for multiple events hosted by other people for different groups of guests to take place at the same times. So you can certainly plan an event with an exclusive VIP list for a smaller group if you wish—or you can be one of the hosts who does extend an open invitation for all.

In this chapter, you'll explore the dos and don'ts related to guest lists for wedding weekend parties and outings, starting with the first and most important one: always consult with the bride and groom for their approval of your guest list so that you don't ruin any event they'd like to plan for themselves.

Who Makes the List

Ideally, every party host will work with the bride and groom—and also consult with parents and other event hosts—to design a coordinated guest list plan for each of the wedding weekend events. The gracious bride and groom will want to be sure that all of their out-of-town guests will have some fun activities to enjoy, and that their various groups of friends and relatives will be able to gather at one or more of the events. So, if you're neither the bride nor the groom, you'll check in with the couple as part of a wider planning circle to be sure that events are planned perfectly and inclusively in the manner the couple wishes. It would be terrible for the bride and groom if a close friend was not invited to a friends-only cocktail party or if a cousin was not invited to a family get-together.

Watch Out!

While most people will bring a bottle of wine, six-pack of beer, food, or desserts to a party as a matter of being proper and gracious guests, don't depend on it. Party hosts who think that people will bring wine so they don't have to buy any have regretted that decision when everyone brought cookie trays or nothing at all, leaving the hosts without a good supply of drinks for their party.

Here's an issue that's going to be a factor: do you only invite out-of-town guests, or do you also invite in-town and otherwise local friends? "We originally planned a pizza party for just the out-of-town friends," says Sarah, a friend of the bride's, "But when local friends heard that our college friends would be coming over that night, they wanted to come to . . . to get time to hang out with friends they haven't seen in years. I could totally understand that. They wanted social time with our Chicago and LA friends, and I didn't want to cost them that, so we just ordered a few more pizzas and let them come." Sarah said that the additional friends she invited did bring bottles of wine and six-packs of beer to the party, so she was helped a bit in that department, too.

A group of friends may be very well defined, such as a group consisting of your college friends and their spouses/significant others, leaving you with very little concern about a guest list for your friends-only party. A get-together with your siblings and cousins also has a circle aspect, removing any concern. It is okay for any crossover guests, such as siblings who would be invited to your party as well as to the parents', to get two invitations and then decide how to divide their time between the two parties. So don't stress about inviting someone if they're also invited elsewhere.

Another solution: you can invite two distinct groups, such as close friends and the cousins, just as the parents might invite their close relatives and their close friends to their own cocktail party.

There are some important guest list trends related to the different and most common wedding weekend events that you can follow.

The Rehearsal Dinner

For the past few years, it was a trend to invite all out-of-town guests to the rehearsal dinner, but that's not the case anymore. In more financially flush years, wedding hosts could afford to double their rehearsal dinner guest list. But in the less affluent times of the past few years, people have gone back to the original model of inviting just immediate family, the bridal party and their guests, the officiant and his or her guest, child attendants and their parents, and those who were taking part in the ceremony plus their dates. That's it.

Since hosts do want to be sure that out-of-town guests are well provided for, they may arrange a cocktail party for those guests to take place at the hotel later in the evening. The bride and groom and others can then head over to the cocktail party after the rehearsal dinner ends. See chapter 8 for full planning details on the rehearsal dinner itself.

The Morning-After Breakfast

The current trend is to host this morning-after breakfast just for the guests who are staying in the hotel. The bridal party may of course be invited, as well as the immediate family, but you do not have to invite other locals or the officiant.

The After-Party

It's now become a trend to extend the celebration after the reception is over, and that often sends the bride, groom, and their close friends and relatives to the hotel bar or lounge for drinks later in the evening. This can be a planned event with invitations sent, or it can be a spontaneous "hey, let's keep the party going" natural progression. Whoever wishes to join the group may do so. But if you wish to host this after-party in your hotel suite or at your home, it's a trend to invite just the bride and groom's closest friends from near and far, plus hand-picked relatives such as close cousins and others who make the bride- and groom-approved VIP list.

Steal My Party Idea

"We invited our friends and close relatives to our after-party, and we also invited the groom's parents and his relatives of our generation since they came in from out of town, and we wanted to include them and get to know them better. It was a lovely evening for all!"—Mathilde, mother of the bride

Parents now tend to plan an after-party at their homes, inviting their friends and close relatives.

Guest List Subtlety Smarts

Since it may turn out that not all guests will be invited to all wedding weekend parties, it's important to practice good diplomacy and subtlety about the events. When you send out an invitation through Evite.com, the people who are invited will be listed on the invitation page, and their responses will be seen by all in that private invitation group. So keep your messaging there, not on Facebook or on Twitter, where all others can see mentions of your party, and where those who are not invited can see them as well, with feelings hurt and awkward messages then sent.

It is okay to let guests know that they're part of an exclusive group invited to the event, and you do appreciate their discretion. How is this done? Add a line to your sent invitation: "We're excited to see you at this private, exclusive party for (bride) and (groom)." gets the message across well. And for invitations going out to close friends, you can use a dash of directness and a splash of humor: "Shhhh! This is a private, exclusive party, so please message us directly, not via Facebook or other social sites. We don't want people crashing:] Thank you!"

Another subtlety strategy is to send out invitations to the after-party a few days before the wedding, not months before. Limiting the amount of time for word to get out often works wonderfully, as does the wording on your days-prior Evite.com invitaion: "Shhh! This is a private party and you're a VIP guest! We can't invite everyone, so this fete is hush-hush!"

Etiquette Friendly

If you'll allow guests to bring a date, you can use the wedding-oriented etiquette addressing of "Susan Jones and Guest" to let Susan know that she can bring a date. If you'd like to limit the plus ones to guests whose significant others are known to you, which is a smart way to limit your guest list, address the invitation to "Susan Jones and Carl Anderson." If no guest is invited, even if others are bringing their significant others, then the invitation just reads, "Susan Jones." If anyone asks if they can bring a date, it's up to you to allow that (if you've had some regrets come in and have the room) or simply say, "I wish I could allow everyone to bring dates, but I have big space and budget restrictions. I'm sorry, but there will be lots of other people there without dates, and you'll have a fantastic time with everyone!"

Avoiding Guest List Overlap and Other Problems

Again, always clear your wished-for guest list with the bride and groom before you mention your party or send out invitations. Even though it can work out fine for some guests to get two or more invitations for simultaneous parties, you never want the wedding couple to feel like you stole their thunder during their wedding weekend by planning your own party to attract their friends and guests, or preventing them from the plans they had in mind. I can't emphasize that enough. Some party hosts have canceled their planned get-togethers when they found out that the bride and groom wanted to plan their own day-after event. It's their weekend, after all.

With guest list overlap handled now, your next focus will be on other guest list issues. For instance, what do you do if you get a call, e-mail, text, or IM from someone who isn't on your party guest list but wants to come anyway? That's a huge etiquette minefield in weddings as a whole, and your party is no different. It's become a bigger problem now that guests seem to be nervier than ever, feeling entitled to invite themselves or bring a guest when no guest was invited. Even parents are extending invitations to others' parties without getting permission first! Yes, manners are not as much of a value now as they used to be, it seems, and as party host you may run into a few ill-mannered people who will get on your list one way or another—or so they plan.

"Can I Come?"

We start with those who ask, sweetly and innocently, perhaps without any intentions of manipulating or perhaps *with* manipulative intentions. No matter the background, the fact remains: you've received a note or call from someone who wants in to your party.

Earlier, you learned the diplomatic response about your limited space and budget if that person can't be invited—or if inviting that person would lead to a chain of additional must invites. So it goes with the dreaded group think of party invitations, that you can't invite Sally without also inviting Jill, Jane, and Jennifer.

If you get that "can I come?" message, again, you can say yes if you have the space and food needed to avoid the hassle and drama of trying to gently let this person down. And as a second tier solution for the pseudo-friend who wants to join the group—perhaps someone whose presence isn't wanted due to dramas she has cooking with other friends on the list, or whose sloppy drunkenness always wrecks a party—a good response is this: "I'm so sorry to have to say no, but we'll see you at the wedding!" I've found that when you don't give an excuse to a pushy person, they have nothing to grab onto and fight you with. If you were to say, "I don't have enough food," for instance (not that that's a good reason to give), that pushy person might say, "Oh, I can bring a platter of my famous meatballs!" or "I'll eat beforehand!" That would lead you into the next downward spiral of this conversation with her. A simple no, and change in subject works best.

"Can I Bring Someone?"

Some people can't go to a party without bringing a date. True, some have social anxieties or don't know anyone else invited and bringing someone would make things more comfortable for them. And some don't want to be the only single there, while others want to show off the hot date they're able to attract. The bottom line is that the pushy request adds another person to your list, another person to feed and supply with drinks, another body in the room.

The solution to this is the blanket answer: "No, I'm sorry, but I don't have the room for everyone to bring dates. I wanted to be sure all the bride and groom's friends could be there, so this party will just be for our circle only, plus a few boyfriends and fiancés that the couple knows." The magic in this response is that you've just preempted the future drama of this guest seeing that other guests have dates at the party, which could otherwise turn into a larger-than-expected crisis later on when she whines about this to the bride.

Etiquette Friendly

If a guest responds that he or she is bringing a date, you're not stuck. Their bad etiquette leads to your next step of proper etiquette in calling this person to say, "I received your RSVP with your plus-one, and I have to let you know that I had to make it a rule that no one brings a date except for very few close couple friends of the bride and groom. So, I'm sorry you can't bring (random guy she added to her RSVP), or everyone at the party is going to be angry with me. Can't make exceptions, and I'm sure you understand. But I'm so excited to see you at the party!" Done!

"Can I Bring My Kids?"

Also in the category of today's nervy guests are the ones who see the bride and groom's weekend as their own chance to show off their kids to their friends, or—less cynically—as their chance to have family and friends meet their kids for the first time. Regardless of intention or nerviness levels, you're the party host, and if guests start requesting to bring their little ones, you're going to have to make your house child friendly and provide a kid-friendly menu. That is, if you choose to allow guests to bring their little ones.

Some wedding weekend events are quite kid friendly, such as trips to museums, festivals, ballgames, or the beach; and others, such as cocktail parties at your home, are less so. So assess your party's style, because it might just be a good thing if you allow friends to bring their kids. Your original plan to have a college friend get-together might just become a more joyous event when everyone has their babies and toddlers with them.

If you're not amenable to any guests bringing their kids along, it's more than okay for you to respond with, "I'm sorry, I've already told lots of guests that this is an adults-only cocktail party, a relaxing night out without the kids." What you might hear, in a parent's well-used method of squeaking by the masses, is that they cannot find a sitter, or that

Steal My Party Idea

"We had so many guests saying they couldn't find a sitter, and we were put in a tough place because of that. But what we did was hire a pair of local teen babysitters to work our party, taking all the kids downstairs to our rec room to entertain them while the adults had a cocktail party upstairs. We got the kids a pizza and cut it into little squares, plus a few other kid food items and cookies, gave the sitter a stack of kid movies to put on the TV, and the little ones had a party of their own downstairs where their parents could just go check on them from time to time. It worked out really well." —Jenni, bridesmaid

they're not comfortable going out without their child. This is a tough one, and few hosts feel comfortable saying, "Well, then, we'll miss you!"

Cancellations

It happens at every party, and also at every wedding. Event coordinators say that it's smart to expect 3 percent of guests to be no-shows or to cancel at the last minute. When your party or outing date gets closer and guests start calling to say they can't make it, it's one of those things that can't be avoided. The one warning I have for you is that it's not proper to tell cancellers that they have to pay for the ticket they won't be using. Just accept the cancellation gracefully and go to your B list of anyone who might like to join in. If it's the night before the event, maybe a close friend would like to invite a date. Maybe a teen would like to bring the friend she originally asked to bring. Don't worry about people being offended that they're a last-second invite—you never know who will be thrilled to get your call.

Cancellations for events that required a ticket,

Etiquette Friendly

When you do make the call to a last-minute invitee, play down the fact that you're calling because someone on your A list just cancelled. Just extend the invitation with a simple, "Would you like to join our group that's going to see (comedian) at the comedy club?" The less you make of the issue, the better.

such as a concert, comedy performance, sporting event, museum, or other ticketed show, present a challenge. If the person prepaid for their ticket and now cancelled, what do you do about refunds? It's a gracious move to offer the canceler his or her money back. They may accept, or they may tell you not to worry about it. That does happen.

Now you have an open ticket. If you have a friend who will join at the last minute, you can decide if you'll ask that person to pay, or—as many hosts do—pick up the cost yourself. Some hosts give the last-minute guest a big discount on the ticket, recouping some of their money.

What's not okay is standing outside the theater with your whole group, trying to scalp that extra ticket.

If you're still considering which type of wedding weekend event to plan, and a ticketed event is on your possibilities list, think about this: how will you handle cancellations and refunds? If you create a list of go-to add-on guests, you might find it to be a nonissue. If the idea of picking up the cost of one or more unused tickets unpleasant, maybe a ticketed event is not the best idea for you.

As for nonticket events, again, cancellations happen and the party goes on as planned!

 **Sending Invitations**

In This Chapter

➤ Sending print invitations or Evites

➤ Wording your invitation

➤ Creating your own invitations

➤ Rules for sending out invitations

Hosts of wedding weekend events approach invitations in either of two mind-sets—quick and easy, or fun and creative craft projects. As I'm sure you know, the quick and easy method is sending invitations online via Evite.com, and the fun and creative craft project method will have you in front of your computer, trying out different layouts, font colors, and graphics as you DIY the print invitations and envelopes to be mailed to guests. This chapter will guide you through both processes, helping you choose the best method for your particular preferences.

But first, keep in mind that it's a must to send invitations to guests—not to depend on spreading the word through parents and friends—so that people clearly know that they're invited and have all the details clearly spelled out for them. The game of Telephone may seem easy, but you'll undoubtedly wind up with guests invited who weren't supposed to be, uninvited guests causing dramas, extra expenses, plans changed and chaotic, and all other manners of headaches.

For many event hosts, making and sending the invitations is one of the most exciting parts of the entire event! Discovering the perfect invitation design, making the perfect invitation design, sharing the design process with a friend or partner, sending out the invitations, and hearing from so many people how awesome they are and how excited they are to attend your bash all add up to a true highlight of your experience! (Brides and grooms say the same thing about their wedding invitation ordering/making/sending/feedback process—it's a thrilling task for them as well!)

Print vs Evite.com

No matter the style of your party—formal dinner party, cocktail party, morning-after breakfast, spa party, and so on—you face the big question: will you mail printed invitations or send them online? It's a rare party host who hasn't seen or heard of Evite.com, so I'll focus just on the pros and cons of that particular method, since even the simplest of common sense factoids can get lost in the flurry of activity you have going on right now, particularly if you're the bride, groom, busy bridal party member, or parent with a ton of other things going on right now. This section will lead you to choose your method, so here are the perks of Evite.com and other online invitation sites to put in your pros column:

Evite.com and Other Online Invitation Providers

Shop Here!

Evite isn't the only online invitation site on the market. It's just become one of those names that's become a verb, its brand is so well known, like Xerox™ or Google. While Evite is popular as an easy, free e-invitation site, look also at Pingg.com for its cute e-invites, and Hallmark.com's easy-to-send freebie e-cards can also be used as e-invitations (just without the visible RSVP list.) Check out the additional e-invitation sites listed in the resources section of this book and you may discover a new favorite!

You've undoubtedly received Evites before or have heard about them. You get an e-mail saying you've been invited to a party, you click on the link, and a cute and colorful invitation with a theme design and pretty font opens up, sharing the party details and giving you a look at who else is going.

As the host, you'll choose from a wide variety of predesigned styles of invitation, from classic and formal to fun and flirty, the soft hues of a spa party, a Vegas-inspired invitation with a roulette wheel and the iconic city sign, and on and on. You might choose a Stylista-type invitation that's purple with a zebra print border, or a Tiffany blue invite perfect for a ladies' tea party. The basic effect is that the designs are already created for you to peruse and choose with just one click. Couldn't be simpler.

Another factor in the pros column for Evite is that it's free. That may be the best perk of all, a savings of $20 or so, including the postage you won't have to use. It also keeps you organized, collecting all RSVPs in one place and tallying a head count of yes, no, and maybe responses. (Most other e-invite and e-card sites do this as well!)

To be fair, let's look at the drawbacks of Evite and other e-invitations.

➤ If you have an outdated e-mail address for a guest, that person might not get her invitation and assume she's been left out. You will have to be sure you have current e-mail addresses for everyone.

➤ Some guests may not have e-mail, and those people will need to get a printout of your invite mailed to them. Even if you know that great-aunt Edna has her grandkids retrieve her e-mails and the like, it's still a proper move on your part to send the print invitation.

➤ Those who are still on the Maybe or Not Yet Responded lists will have to be called for their RSVP. It's a sad fact that many people forget to RSVP or just don't commit because some better plan may come along and they want to keep their options open. Or, the Evite e-mail got deleted or lost in their high-traffic e-mail accounts. As host, you get to hunt them down—but this is the same con that's part of the print invitation territory.

Steal My Party Idea

"Since the bride and groom are really eco-friendly, living a green lifestyle, I knew they'd appreciate my sending out e-invitations that didn't require any use of paper or inks. So that's why I chose to do e-invites for the party I was throwing for them."—Carole, bridesmaid

Etiquette Friendly

Don't let opinionated others talk you out of e-invitations, saying it's not good etiquette to send an e-invite for any wedding weekend event. There are lots of people out there on message boards sharing their opinions of what's proper and what's not, according to how they've always done things or what's in their e-book etiquette manifesto on sale for $29.99. Forget the noise. You can send e-invites for wedding weekend celebrations and events—even for the rehearsal dinner and morning-after breakfast; just not for a formal wedding ceremony or reception, which is almost always best suited for a formal print invitation. Everything else is fair game for an easy, free e-invitation if this method works for you and for the guest list.

Print Invitations

We start off with a very big entry for the pros column: print invitations are fun and exciting to order or make, and they're such a thrill to get in the mail! A pretty little envelope showing up in the mailbox gives guests a tangible little treat to hold onto and admire. They appreciate the work it took to create it and at the same time looking forward to the event to come. As fun as it is to get an e-invitation, it's just not the same type of thrill.

Another important perk to print invitations: they become fabulous, fun keepsakes for the bride and groom, parents, and the party hosts. Those lovely little cards in those stylish colors, with bows on top or buckles on the ribbon tie, modern fonts or pearlized borders go right into the bride's scrapbook or photo album, becoming a part of her time capsule of wonderful moments from her wedding weekend. In contrast, she could print out a copy of the Evite page—which many couples do—but that printout isn't going to look as nice on the refrigerator.

"Our circle of friends has done so many Evites for so many different kinds of parties, as great as they are, we've all seen the best designs before," says Kimberly, a bridesmaid for a fall wedding. "So sending out a cute printed invitation gave it that 'something different' that impressed the bride and made my part of the planning process a little more special and recognized than just being the person who set up the Evite page." Kimberly says that she and her friends use Evite all the time for birthday parties, showers, bachelorette parties, and other events, and by virtue of doing a print invite for her party, it looked like she spent a fortune and went above and beyond for the bride and groom, when it was really quite simple to arrange. So there's your next pros column entry: a print invitation can be an attention-getting change of pace from your group's usual invitation method.

Watch Out!

For any professionally ordered invitation or print item, always be sure to look at the minimum amount you can order. If you have a thirty-person guest list for your event, you don't want to waste time or money when you discover that the style you want is only available in a minimum order of one hundred cards.

The creative angle of choosing pretty card stocks or colored papers, pearlized borders, vellums, imported papers, eco-papers, and other style elements turns you into a designer for a day, and that's another perk of going with print invitations. You get to decide if your signature look will be a single-panel traditional card, an origami-like foldout, a modern square single panel, a pop-up or any number of other options. You get to impress with your invitation design acumen, which is all the more special in our current world of 2-D online invites.

Check out the resources section for a list of invitation sites, where you can browse through thousands of invitation styles and brand-name collections, and where you may fall in love with a print design that works perfectly for your planned party.

The world of fill-in-the-blank print invitations has made a return to cute, chic, stylish designs lately, so don't count out the concept of write-in cards. The designs from PSAEssentials.com are especially style savvy, and you'll find a wide array of theme-oriented fill-in cards at affordable stores like Target, WalMart, Kmart, and other big-box stores. Hosts of activity-centric parties say that they're getting great prices on, say, bowling-themed or football-themed invitations meant for kids' birthday parties, only the hosts are filling them out with their weekend theme party event info.

And, of course, there's the hot trend of sending printed postcards in regular (5.47" x 4.21") or oversized (8.5" x 5.47") designs, which gives you the creativity of a front image and wording, plus easy-to-read details on the back of the card. Brides and grooms are flocking to inexpensive postcard design sites like Vistaprint.com to get fifty or so high-quality glossy postcards for under $10, or even less with a great sale.

Money Mastery

Packs of fill-in cards are ultra-inexpensive at stores like Target, Walmart, and Kmart, as well as at your local craft chain, and with 20 percent off in-store or online coupons found at RetailMeNot.com—which will point out stores' current sales—you'll get your one, two, or three packs of invites for a very low cost. I also like to look in the dollar bins at craft stores and at Target, as well as at dollar stores, for fabulously inexpensive yet still cute invitation packs.

Invitation Wording

An invitation shares the what, when, where that guests need to know, but there's also room to have some fun with the wording, get punny with the party theme and use some humor, and otherwise make the invitation to your unique event stand out. For more formal events, such as the rehearsal dinner, your invitation wording will of course be more formal and proper, adhering to the rules of etiquette that dictate wedding invitation and envelope wording.

In the upcoming chapters, you'll find samples of invitation wording to copy or use as inspirational jumping-off points for your own custom wording for each type of party, event, and outing listed here by theme. For instance, a planned trip into the big city for a girls' shopping spree might call forth your circle of friends' love for designer brands, so your invitation—featuring icon-stamped shopping bags and an illustration of stylish friends shopping their hearts out or stepping out of a limo—can announce the indulgent day with "Manolo. Chanel. Gucci. We're hitting them all during Katie's New York City girls' shopping spree," and so on.

The All-Important RSVP

No invitation is complete without a rock solid RSVP, providing one or more contacts and a specific deadline for responding. The easier you make it for guests to RSVP, the more likely you are to get them to RSVP and not have to call people a week before your party to ask if they're coming or not. So follow this model of wise RSVP wording and contact provision:

> To help us in our planning, we ask that you RSVP
> by May 16th at the very latest
> Contact us at:
> Carole: carolesmith@domainname.net, 973-555-0000
> Mike: mikensmith@domainname.net, 973-555-1111
> Thank you!

Carole and Mike provided both their e-mail addresses and cell numbers, and their RSVP request mentioned "to help us with our planning." That's a subtle reminder to guests that their responses are important for hosts' shopping lists and other plans. The "Thank you!" at the bottom is a touch of class.

In some regions of the country, it's customary to print on invitations, "Regrets only," signaling to guests that they should contact you only if they can't make it to your event. Those who don't reply, you assume, will be there. Now if your party is the type that requires

Watch Out!

The number one and number two rules when it comes to invitation wording are:

➤ Make sure all details are 100 percent correct, from start times to addresses to URLs, and all other essentials.

➤ Make sure everything is spelled correctly, from names to locations to the smallest words in every sentence. For instance, printing your when it should be you're is a glaring error that guests catch and your invitation effect is thus ruined.

a solid head count in advance so that you can order catering or make your own menu or buy tickets or know how many people will fit in a limo or party bus, etc., it's wise not to specify "Regrets only." When money is on the line, not to mention the clear information needed to plan an event well, it's a must to know exactly who's coming and who's not. So buck the regrets only trend with a message of:

> We require RSVPs for this very special party
> in honor of Samantha and James.
> Please do contact us by May16th at the very latest,
> so that we can plan the best celebration ever for the happy couple!

To get results, you have to be direct. Not dictatorial, as in, "If you don't RSVP, we won't let you in," but firm enough to get the point across that responses are needed and expected by a certain date.

If after all your efforts and inserts some guests still do not RSVP, your most efficient course of action is to call them directly, as host, to get their yes or no. This most often delivers results, but in this hectic era, some people still hesitate and say they're not sure if they can make it. With no definitive answer, your best bet is to build enough into your menu to accommodate a handful of extra guests who do show up. If you're like me, you cater to feed an army, so that shouldn't be a problem. (I also cater my parties to provide lots of take-homes for guests and leftovers for us, so consider that for your own self-catering configurations.) If your event is a per-person booking at a restaurant that needs an exact head count, tell the stalling guest, "I understand that your weekend is hectic, but the restaurant is giving us only until Tuesday to give a final head count for the party, and after that date it's going to cost us a big extra fee to make any changes." Once people know there's a financial loss on the line, they often make a best effort to deliver an answer. (There's no need to say how much the financial loss would be, just hint at one, and you'll be fine.)

Etiquette Friendly

For more formal events, such as the rehearsal dinner, you can insert a response card—with return postage already on the little envelope—into your print invitation mailing as a prompt for guests to send in their RSVPs. This little response card tells guests that you're serious and they have to RSVP.

If you're going with print invitations—rather than e-invitations through a site that tallies your RSVPs automatically and points out who hasn't responded yet—create an organized spreadsheet that lets you keep track of who's RSVP'd and who has yet to contact you. This one step, pure organization, saves you time, money, stress, and last-minute hassles.

Making Invitations

Taking on the task of making invitations for your get-together means you get to flex those creative muscles, choose hues, write wonderful wording, and otherwise design the invitations that will show up like little presents in guests' mailboxes.

Those who DIY invitations do so in one of two ways: they either design simply, using the fonts and graphic design options in their home computer's Word program, or they use invitation-making software.

No-Fuss Word Processor Invitation Design

Simply done, an invitation designed in a Word program can be made full page with borders, shading, a fabulous font announcing the party details, graphics inserted, and so on. Your printer program then steps in to give you the option of printing one, two, or four invitations to a page, and your slipped-in card stock becomes the foundation for your homemade invitations. Given the improved nature of computer clip art, more ornate fonts, and an expanded range of colors for fill and font shadings, it's possible to design any style of invitation from an elegant black-and-white theme to a girlie pink tea party invitation with an actual pink feather glued onto the image of a party hat, a gridiron football-themed invitation for your at-home play-off game-viewing party, and all manner of other celebrations theme-perfect invitation.

Steal My Party Idea

"All of the other co-hosts looked in on my design file through Google Documents, which is a file-sharing free system that lets far-apart groups work together on an important project. I designed the invitation, let everyone know it was there, they logged in, shared their design thoughts with me, and in a snap, I made the adjustments and we were done!"—Danielle, bridesmaid and co-host of the after-party

Invitation-Making Software and Kits

They're inexpensive, they're easy, and your investment in an invitation-making software program delivers perks for any future parties or events you'll host, since you can use it again and again for holiday cocktail parties, baby showers, kids' birthdays, and so on. The current class of invitation-making software has evolved so much over the programs launched just a few years ago. Now you'll find invitation-making software kits for under $30, with hundreds of different templates, thousands of different clip art graphics, tons of different fonts, modern classic style designs, theme designs, trendy colors, and even packs of invitation papers and envelopes for your print project.

Check out the resources section to find where you can get invitation-making software kits, such as Mountaincow.com's inexpensive wedding- and party-themed software programs, papers, and even tools that let you print out official postage to coordinate with the design of your invitations! In the craft store, you'll find Martha Stewart's popular line of invitation-making software, as well.

In addition to easy design templates, invitation-making software makes printing easy to arrange, offering you the option of single-panel card printing, dual-fold greeting card style, or postcard printouts, among other styles and sizes. It will show you where you're over the line into borders, and it will show you where to pop out holes at the top of your invitation if you want to make a ribbon-tie accent. The designers have thought of everything.

Money Mastery

If you're part of the wedding-planning circle—bride or groom, maid of honor, bridesmaid, parents—look at invitation-making software as a fabulous tool to be used many times in the wedding-planning process. If you buy it, or make it a group-share purchase with the other bridesmaids, everyone gets to use it for their own print projects for this wedding—and access it in the future as well!

Accents, Ribbons, and Bows

Invitations are getting dressed up like dolls these days, with ribbons, bows, sparkles, stick-on crystals, dangling charms, and all manner of additional add-ons to make print invites stand out. As you'll see in the next chapter, even the wedding weekend itineraries are getting the same accented treatment as invitations, being beaded, bowed, sparkled, and sequined as an extra effect.

Your theme party or party style will inspire many different fun accents for your invitations as well as for place cards and other print items that will play a part in your big event. For instance, retro fuzzy stickers of soccer balls can dress up your invitation card inviting families to a backyard soccer skills contest. Stick-on hot-pink Swarovski crystal dots can make invitation cards stand out for an old-fashioned sleepover or Barbie™-themed girls' only party. Again, you'll find accent ideas in each of the upcoming chapters, both from me and from real-life party hosts whose décor ideas are sure to impress.

Keep in mind, though, that raised accents mean each invitation will need to be specially packaged, and at the very least hand-canceled at the post office due to its raised and bumpy surface that mail processing machinery can't handle (and may chew up!). So putting any kind of raised accent on your invites means you have to stand in line at the post office.

Steal My Party Idea

"To get everyone excited about our 1920s-themed cocktail party, we inserted into the invitation a little printed photo from the movie The Great Gatsby, just so they'd be able to see the style of dress and décor from that era."—Lisa, bridesmaid

"We decided to give everyone a little pre-favor—a cocktail recipe card—in their invitation, so that everyone attending and not attending would get a little something fun!"—Mandy, bride

Inserts in Print Invitations

Use the same invitation-making software, with matching fonts and ink colors, to create a coordinated look among your invite and any inserts such as maps, driving direction sheets, game cards (such as trivia or recipe to be filled out by guests and handed in for a theme event), response cards (if you wish for that formal RSVP method) and other items. By *coordinated*, we're talking paper stock and color, ink color, font style, and graphics.

Invitation Etiquette

Etiquette may be a bit more relaxed for wedding weekend events than it remains for the wedding itself, but no matter the event, it's still smart to follow basic rules of proper decorum when writing out and sending invitations. Here are the basic bridal etiquette rules that are best to follow, no matter what your party or outing style or formality:

➤ Send one invitation to each couple (married, engaged, dating), not separate cards for dating couples while other "official" couples get a card together—that hurts feelings.

➤ If a couple's kids are invited, write, "Mr. and Mrs. Jeffrey Smith and Family" on the envelope, so that the Smiths know the kids are invited. An inner envelope, should you choose to use one, can be titled with the couple's names and the names of each child.

➤ Send a separate invitation for each guest over age sixteen.

➤ If you'll grant an "and guest" for any single guest, it's okay to write "and guest" if you don't know—and have no way of finding out—the significant other's name.

➤ If you can find out the significant other's name, it's proper to write that name on the invitation along with the known-to-you guest's name.

➤ Handwritten envelopes are considered more proper and more formal than ones with printed labels on them. So for the rehearsal dinner, morning-after breakfast, and other more formal events, hand address the envelopes. For other get-togethers, labels are acceptable.

➤ If you're sending invitations via e-mail, send them with a "viewed" or "received" receipt so that you know the recipient got his or her invitation. It is etiquette friendly to do so.

➤ Send invitations to wedding weekend events as early as possible so that out-of-town guests can make plans to stay an extra day or take an earlier flight into town in order to attend. Invitations sent four to six months prior are quite common and are more etiquette friendly than invitations sent a week before the wedding, when it's too late for guests to adjust their travel and lodging plans.

➤ Requesting RSVPs via e-mail is perfectly fine, etiquette-wise, for your wedding weekend event—even for rehearsal dinners.

➤ Mention nothing about gifts or gift registries on any invitation. The only proper place for mention of gift registries is in bridal shower invitations.

CHAPTER 6

Wedding Weekend Itineraries

> ## In This Chapter
>
> ➤ Putting your itinerary together
>
> ➤ Designing your itinerary
>
> ➤ Distributing your itineraries

Among the many pretty printed items in a wedding celebration is a gorgeous wedding weekend itinerary, which you can help create in design and content. If you're the bride or groom, you're chief designer of this document that lists all of the inclusive parties, wedding events, and outings taking place during the weekend of your wedding. If you're a host of one or more events, you get to consult and perhaps even take on the design and printing of these itinerary pages.

In this chapter, you'll learn all about what does and doesn't go on a wedding weekend itinerary, what the new musts are, how to make the itineraries in fine style, and how to get them into guests' hands.

Here's what a wedding itinerary looks like:

> The Wedding Weekend of Carla and Dan
>
> Friday, June 5th: Welcome Cocktail Party
> 6 pm
> At the hotel lounge
> Dress is casual
>
> Saturday, June 6th: The Wedding and Reception
> 1 pm
>
> Saturday, June 6th: The After-Party
> 9 pm
> At the hotel lounge
> Wear your wedding clothes or change into casual dress
>
> Sunday, June 7th: Morning-After Breakfast
> 9 am
> At the hotel restaurant
> Dress is casual
>
> Sunday, June 7th: Softball Tournament and Cookout
> 1 pm
> Game: At Johnson Park, 1 Main Street
> Cookout: At Lila and Mike's house, 314 Hickory Place
> Dress to play, and bring a bathing suit for the poolside cookout!
> Hosts: Lila and Mike, 202-555-9765 for directions and RSVP
>
> We look forward to celebrating with you!

Of course, your itinerary will be custom styled with your event details included. Read on to discover the additional musts and tips for creating an outstanding itinerary.

What to Include

It's quite simple, actually. You'll provide the date, time, and location for each clearly defined event. For any event that takes place outside of the hotel grounds—such as at someone's house—you'll provide the hosts' names and phone number for RSVPs and more information.

Here are some additional musts for your itinerary:

➤ Dress code: Let guests know if they can wear jeans, or if a location has a no-jeans policy. For instance, your itinerary block might read like this:

> Sunday, June 7th: Afternoon Tea
> 3 pm
> At the hotel lobby
> No jeans, please.
> Dresses or khakis and sweaters are preferred for women;
> jackets for men.

➤ Additional outfits needed: If swimming will be available at a cookout, beach, or amusement park, alert guests to the need for bathing suits and cover-ups.

➤ Host contact information: As mentioned, provide the hosts' phone number, but not their work number, or an e-mail address that they may prefer to keep private. Ask (if the host is not you) which number they prefer guests to use, home or cell.

➤ RSVP deadlines: Hosts of parties and ticketed outings will need plenty of advance notice so that they can arrange for catering, rentals, ticket orders, and other essentials. A good rule of thumb is to provide an RSVP deadline that's at least three weeks before the date of the event.

Etiquette Friendly

Only include events to which all guests are invited, since it would be brutally rude to list fun-sounding outings with a designation of private party on them. Those private parties get their own invitations and are left off of this document.

➤ Any expenses required: If you or the host will not pick up the expense of tickets to a show or exhibit, you need to provide that information here, just as you did in the original invitation. Here's how it would look:

> Sunday, June 7th: Afternoon at the Museum
> 2 pm
> Museum of Local History
> Ticket prices are $12 for adults, $6 for children aged 6 through 17, free for children under age 6
> Please contact event host Tania Ridgemeyer, 212-555-8754 if you would like to join our group.

That payment information is just a reminder of what was in the invitation. When guests see on the itinerary that a group is already going, they can call the host to make arrangements to pay and join the fun.

> ➤ Street address: For any private home or establishment, provide the street address with town and zip code so that guests can enter that data into their vehicle navigation systems, easily finding the location of the event during the wedding weekend without you having to distribute printed driving directions to guests.

> ➤ URL of the establishment: Especially for restaurants, a glimpse into where everyone's going allows guests to check out the menu (and its prices!) so that they know what to expect when they get there.

> ➤ Additional information: Include other pertinent information such as where parking is located, if the site doesn't have a parking lot, or—if you're all headed on a highway to get to the locale—the need for coins or toll road passes.

How to Make Your Itineraries

Brides and grooms still want printed itineraries to slip into their guests' welcome baskets or to mail prior to the wedding day. Yes, they often do feature this information on their personal wedding website, but part of the fun of wedding preparations is making pretty, tangible products that thrill guests and also become keepsakes later on. So making itineraries is one of the top DIY projects shared by brides and grooms or taken on by a helpful volunteer (perhaps you.)

You don't need special software to create an itinerary. Your word processor provides all of the design capabilities, fonts, and fill colors you could possibly need, and you have a world of graphics and clip art at your disposal. Take Microsoft Word, for example. With it, you can center, italicize, change the sizes of your fonts, insert images, fill blocks, create borders, and more. Your itinerary design depends on your creativity.

Brides and grooms may chime in, asking for their personalized monogram to be placed at the top of the page. They paid to have it designed for their

Money Mastery

Ink is expensive, so design your itineraries to avoid large blocks of colored ink such as box filler, as seen in the gray box fill on the previous pages of this chapter. When your printer has to fill large spaces such as these boxes or big graphics with ink, it costs more, and it comes out not so pretty when big, colored portions look wavy from being wetted with so much ink. Keep color to thin borders and font colors, and use tiny images or accents only.

invitations and programs, and they'd love to carry that print theme all the way through to the itinerary. So that shall be done, as they wish.

Follow the model at the start of this chapter to line up your events in chronological order, making sure that fonts are large and clear enough to read. Some decorative fonts can become quite tricky to decipher, and some numbers can be tough to read. A "0" can look like a "9" in some fonts, so be sure to test out your itinerary in its design form, and ask a third party to read it over for legibility and for grammar and typos, before you send your design to the bride and groom for their okay—an essential step—or else you might waste valuable paper and ink while printing out a version that meets with displeasure or has a schedule conflict or a mistake in it.

Now let's get into design and creation.

Design and Style

Simply put, the simpler the better. You can get artsy and wild with color, with a patterned border, and with a great graphic on top or bottom of the page, but always stick to the ratio of 20 percent of the page being decorative and 80 percent featuring an unencumbered view of your wording.

Choose your color scheme to match the color of the welcome guest baskets or bags that the bride and groom choose, since it looks so much better to have a coordinated package. So if the welcome bag is a tangerine color, your itinerary can be shaded in tangerine, brighter orange, and a light yellow. Here are some additional color blend ideas:

➤ If the bag is a light green, your itinerary can be shaded in light sage and hunter green.

➤ If the bag is bright pink, your itinerary can be shaded in bright pink to match, plus two shades of lighter pink, and also white.

➤ If the bag is lavender, your itinerary can be shaded in matching lavender and deep purple.

➤ If the bag is light blue, your itinerary can be shaded in light blue, cobalt blue and silver for sparkle.

With your color palette chosen, now it's time to pick your paper shade. Go to an office supply store for the best color variety and pricing on standard 8-1/2" x 11" paper stock. You can go a bit heavier in paper stock than the usual 20-pound computer paper to give your itinerary a slightly sturdier feel, just a bit more flexible than a manila folder. Glossy paper may seem like a good idea for decorative effect, but some inks can smear on glossy paper, so test your own supply before investing.

At the office supply store you'll find reams of paper in light blue, lavender, soft pink, and in neon oranges and blues, purples, and reds, as well as theme-décor papers featuring everything from zebra-print borders to snowflakes to kittens, horses, and red-white-and-blue Fourth of July motifs. You will see in the craft store the same kinds of décor paper in brand names and in unique shapes such as square card stock or heart-shaped card stock. With your papers chosen, you can now design your layout.

Keep your itinerary list to a centered strip of entries, and for ease of reading, use one size font for the event name and a slightly smaller size font for the details. It might look like this:

> Sunday, June 7th: Afternoon Tea
> 3 pm
> In the hotel lobby

The effect is subtle, but guests' eyes register the event names first, scanning down to assess the lineup of available activities and outings. Stick to just two font sizes—no more—or else your itinerary will look cluttered and like you're trying too hard, without a pleasing design aesthetic.

The wedding's season may also play a part in the itinerary design. Take a winter wedding, for instance. The itinerary may look like this:

> Friday, December 12th: Welcome Ice Skating Party
> 7 pm
> At the Wollman Rink
> Followed by drinks and cocktail party fare at the hotel

Your design for this winter itinerary could be light blue paper with white and silver snowflakes, or festive red paper with silver print and white and silver snowflakes. A summertime itinerary could feature a sandy beach bottom with a blue Caribbean ocean scene and palm trees, with your itinerary wording at the center of the page.

Your events don't always have to be lined up down the center of the page. They do need to stay in chronological order, but they can be aligned as such:

Sunday, June 7th:
Afternoon Tea
3pm
Hotel Lobby

        Ladies' Spa Afternoon
        4 pm
        Salon Aurore

                Cocktail Party

7 pm
Sue & Fred's House
9 Oak Street, Millville 06553
459-555-0000

You're the artist of your itinerary, and layout is up to your wishes, accented by your choices of borders and art accenting.

Borders and Accenting

The simplest of itinerary designs, with event information centered and printed in a pretty font, can use just a touch of border and accenting for artistic flair. If going too far with design is a mistake, so is going too plain and unadorned. So use your home computer's graphic design system to play with different borders and box outlines to surround your itinerary wording. Here are some examples that I created in less than two seconds using my own Word program:

```
The Wedding Weekend of Carla and Dan

Friday, June 5th: Welcome Cocktail Party
6 pm
At the hotel lounge
Dress is casual

Saturday, June 6th: The Wedding and Reception
1 pm
```

```
The Wedding Weekend of Carla and Dan

Friday, June 5th: Welcome Cocktail Party
6 pm
At the hotel lounge
Dress is casual

Saturday, June 6th: The Wedding and Reception
1 pm
```

And so on. I just clicked on Borders and Shading, and these two designs popped out at me. You can then choose the option of filling these boxes with any color shade you desire, and with a few extra taps on the keyboard, you can arch your top line of text to fit the couple's pretty monogram right beneath their names.

Speaking of design elements at the top of the page, an easy DIY method of accenting printed wedding weekend itineraries is the decorative hole punch. Take a walk down that particular aisle of a craft store and you'll be amazed by the hole punches that pop out small, medium, and large stars, hearts, circles, little brides and grooms, butterflies, wildly intricate snowflakes, and other designs that look laser cut (similar to those pricy laser-cut wedding invitations out there). Choose your theme hole punch design, and then pop out accents in the following patterns that designers say work best to avoid that home-done look.

➤ A cluster of three to five hole punches in the lower right-hand corner of the itinerary

➤ An evenly spaced line of five to six hole punches along just the bottom edge of the itinerary

➤ A single large hole punch in the upper right-hand corner of the itinerary

➤ A single large hole punch, surrounded by a half-dozen mini-hole punches of the same shape (like stars) in the upper right-hand corner of the itinerary

➤ For a color pop, punch out your design on the itinerary card, and place a colored sheet of paper behind the itinerary card so that your hole punches reveal that hue.

➤ Use your hole punch on the bottom right or left corners of an *envelope* and place your folded, colored itinerary sheet inside the envelope so that the color 'pop' is visible from the outside.

And then there's the accenting touch of tying little ribbon bows at the top of the itinerary card. Pop two small holes at the center top of the page, and feed the ends of a 4-inch length of color-coordinated ribbon from the back to the front of the card. Tie the ribbon ends into a small bow, and there you have it!

At a craft store, you'll find sheets of stick-on Swarovski crystals in tiny circles, stars, hearts, and other shapes in a range of colors from clear to pastel to bright. Carefully peel and stick these crystals onto your itinerary in a starburst or other design in a corner or along a bottom, top, or side edge of the card.

Watch Out!

Since you'll be playing with the layout of your carefully worded itinerary, save your original Word document in a separate file to keep it safe. When effects are being added and deleted, you never know when a block of text can sneak its way into your highlight for deletion. This safe extra step keeps your master wording safe and separate from your design document, and you can go back into it to copy any wiped-away text as your design process continues. Save your designed document in a separate file, such as CarlaandDansItineraryfinal.pdf.

How to Distribute Itineraries

The most common distribution method of printed itinerary sheets or square cards is placing them in the welcome gift bags or baskets that each of the out-of-town guests will receive when checking into their hotel rooms. The itinerary serves as a pretty and fun addition to a well-packed welcome basket, and guests have on hand an easy reference to the events and locations taking place throughout the weekend.

You can also hand out these cards at the guest welcome cocktail party, or arrange them on a side table for guests to take on their own.

Guests who are not staying at the hotel may receive these via regular mail, or you can send the pdf file to them via e-mail. Don't forget to present these itinerary cards to the bride and groom as well as to their family members so that they may use them and keep them as wonderful keepsakes!

Watch Out!

Don't go crazy with these stick-ons, or your itinerary will look like a preschool craft project. Less is more. One edge of the card is perfect for a line or squiggle of crystals, not all edges.

PART TWO

Wedding Weekend Event Categories

CHAPTER 7

 # Welcome Cocktail Parties

In This Chapter

➤ Where to have the party

➤ What to serve

➤ Planning the party

In chapter 2, you started thinking about arrival cocktail parties with your focus on the timing of this, the most common first celebration of the weekend. It's become a fabulous trend to welcome out-of-town guests with a lovely cocktail party taking place as they're checking into their hotel. Unlike all of the events hosted for the bride and groom, this one is for the guests to welcome them in style, treat them to delicious party fare and cocktails after their long and arduous travels, and—perhaps most importantly—make it easy for them to meet up with friends and relatives who are also arriving that day.

When guests arrive at the hotel, they find upon checking in the usual guest goodie bag filled with snacks, drinks, and spa items, but they also receive a printed invitation card instructing them to "join us in the Garden Room for a welcome cocktail party from 3 pm to 5 pm!" Since so many guests spend money on plane tickets, train tickets, tanks of gas, and other travel expenses—not to mention perhaps taking a day off of work to be present at your Friday night wedding—this invitation is quite a delight, and the party is a thoughtful and appreciated event.

This chapter will inspire you to plan a unique and creative welcome cocktail party for arriving wedding guests. You'll consider different types of locations for this event, plan a pleasing menu and drinks list, and arrange the additional details that bring this notable first celebration of the wedding to life. The bride and groom have entrusted you with the first mood-setting party of their big weekend, so it has to be a good one. Read on to discover the smart planning strategies and creative touches to make your arrival cocktail party a standout success.

Watch Out!

An important factor to keep in mind is that there doesn't have to be just one party for all arriving guests. While the all-inclusive welcome party is indeed the most common occurrence, the bride and groom might host one for their bridal party members earlier in the afternoon (or the evening before), parents might host welcome parties at their houses for their arriving friends and family, local relatives might host one, and so on. So if it is your wish to host the welcome cocktail party, don't be shocked if you learn that the bride and groom or the parents have a separate event planned at the same time. If you're the bride and groom, it's wise to send your invitations to your hosted welcome party out quite early, so that other relatives and friends can make their plans around yours.

Locations

The majority of welcome cocktail parties take place at the hotel where the guests are staying, since it's the most convenient location for them, a relief at the end of their journey. This section will help you look around the hotel establishment to find the perfect on-site location for your party.

Talk with the hotel's special events manager to arrange an established welcome cocktail party, no matter where you plan to host it on the hotel property. The manager can often provide you with extra perks and freebies on your menu, and also help you with the challenge of providing an open bar tab for a large circle of guests without having the total spiral out of control. "Our manager understood that we were concerned about the etiquette of closing the bar tab down at 5 pm, since we didn't want to offend anyone, and she offered to save the day by coming in and telling our guests that she hoped everyone had a wonderful time, but they now have to clear out our space for another incoming party group," says Maria, a bridesmaid. "I *loved* it that the hotel manager was so great at handling this kind of party danger zone, and no one was the least bit offended!"

The Hotel Lounge

Your group gathers in a reserved corner of the lounge, complete with velvet ropes and a Private Party sign. Some lounges have separate party rooms with leather chairs and banquettes, big-screen televisions, and other upscale amenities.

Or, your group can simply take over a section of tables by the bar, with your circle of guests growing naturally as each couple and each family arrives. Rounds of drinks come to your tables, appetizer platters are ordered, and your cocktail party evolves naturally.

A Hotel Suite

For a small circle of guests, a hotel suite provides the perfect upscale setting for a welcome cocktail party, especially if the suite is a lavish one with a separate living room, wet bar, and a fabulous view. Hosts who throw private VIP welcome parties—such as ones for the bridal party members—appreciate the privacy afforded in a hotel suite setting, where they can celebrate freely without worrying about other wedding guests joining their circle, swelling the bar tab.

Money Mastery

If guests will be staying at two or three different hotels, chosen to suit their budgets or to match their existing hotel membership plans, research the two or three different locations to see which establishment will give you special wedding group discounts. It may be the main hotel where the wedding will take place, where a large block of hotel rooms are booked by the wedding guests. That locale may give you a fabulous cut-rate price since you're with a group that's spending a good chunk of money on its property.

Or just by asking, you might get a fantastic deal for the use of the back terrace and gardens at the bed-and-breakfast where a smaller number of guests are staying. It pays in savings when you spend time researching and mentioning that yours is a wedding group event. Many locales offer impressive discounts for such special events.

Another perk of the hotel suite setting is that you can set up a buffet of hors d'oeuvre platters on the bartop, and a self-serve bar on the countertop, and your small circle of guests can help themselves to your offerings. You don't need to worry about strangers dining from your private buffet, as you might find happening at a cocktail party set up in a corner of the hotel's lounge.

A Hotel Party Room

Most hotels are able to close sliding wall partitions in their large banquet rooms to create a smaller party room, or they may have a line of small private party rooms on, say, the second floor of the hotel. These are the private event rooms booked for small celebrations as well as for corporate meetings, seminars, and other professional events. It doesn't cost a lot to reserve one of these private meeting/party rooms, and they may be the perfect size for the twenty guests you're inviting to the party, just a tad too many to invite to a hotel room or suite.

You can decorate these party rooms, and the catering is handled by the hotel's special events staff and chefs.

The Hotel's Outdoor Areas

Ask the hotel's events manager if you can host your welcome cocktail party in any of the hotel's outdoor gathering areas. Bear in mind, though, that another cocktail party may be booked at the hotel's poolside area or in its private, flowering tree-filled courtyard, veranda, or atrium. So before you court disaster by inviting guests to join your party poolside, make sure you'll definitely have access to the hotel's poolside the night before the wedding. You must book the space far in advance to be sure it will be open to your guests and that you'll be welcome to socialize there.

Steal My Party Idea

"Our fireplace was the deciding factor on where we'd have our welcome cocktail party. On the chilly evening before the winter wedding, we set a roaring fire in the fireplace, served hot mulled wine and appetizers, and created a ski chalet feeling for guests to relax in."—Emily, bridesmaid

At Home

Guests check into the hotel at 3 pm and by 5 pm they're relaxing at your place with a glass of wine in hand. Some, again, may have had a long travel day, starting in the early hours of the morning, and it's just far more comfortable and relaxing to socialize in your home.

Party hosts say they love welcoming their friends and relatives into their homes, to show off their interior décor, and to make babysitting issues easier on them. The kids just stay downstairs or up in their rooms as the adults socialize, or the kids are entirely welcome to join in the festivities, meet the guests, even hand out the cookies and cupcakes they made as their contribution to the party.

Another selling factor for the at-home party: your catering may be more appetizing and healthier than bar food platters available at the hotel lounge. The bar menu at the hotel may feature fried calamari, nachos, potato skins, and buffalo wings, and your at-home menu may include veggie-filled dishes, steamed spring rolls, five-grain warm rolls right out of the oven, and other light bites that guests enjoy fully at the start of a wedding weekend when they're sure to indulge in less diet-friendly foods.

A smart party–planning note: since guests will have to travel to your home, set the party time for a few hours after hotel check-in so that guests don't feel rushed and can shower before coming to your place.

Menu and Drinks

As mentioned, cocktail fare may be light and healthy such as those veggie-filled spring rolls and veggie platters with an array of light dips, or it may be a mix of veggie dishes and some traditional finger foods such as pigs in a blanket and easy-to-serve bar food platters at the hotel lounge. In this section, you'll think about the menu you wish to offer guests with an eye toward making budget-friendly choices that still look as if you spent a lot more.

Buffet Platters

The easiest way to provide food for guests who may be arriving over the course of several hours is to set out at least six different platters of edibles on a decorated buffet table. With a pile of plates and help-yourself utensils, guests can pick and choose from your smartly planned buffet offerings.

The top platters for a welcome cocktail party buffet include:

➤ Vegetable crudite platter with a range of dips, from ranch to sour cream and onion, and salsa

➤ Mini sandwiches or half-wraps filled with roast beef and cheese, turkey, grilled veggies with a balsamic vinaigrette, or simple mozzarella and tomato slices

➤ Crackers and hummus, including gourmet flavors such as roasted red pepper and jalapeno spice

➤ Water crackers and flavored Italian crackers, or low-fat wheat crackers

➤ Chips and salsa bar

➤ Spring rolls and gyoza filled with veggies, pork, or chicken, with soy and wasabi dipping sauces

➤ Baked appetizers, such as those crowd-favorite pigs in a blanket, spinach puffs, chili-filled puffs, potato skins, egg rolls, coconut shrimp, and other items easily found in the freezer section of your supermarket, if not ordered in platter form at the hotel's lounge

➤ Hot chafing dishes from which guests scoop a few barbecue or teriyaki meatballs, as well as other hotplate dishes, including artichoke and spinach dips with melty cheese and fondue-type cheese sauces that guests can spoon over their crisp, raw veggies

➤ Artistically cut and garnished fruit platters filled with mango slices arranged in fans, pineapple bites, and more

Money Mastery

Seafood dishes might seem like an indulgent way to treat arriving guests, but those shrimp cocktail bites and salmon cakes are often very expensive, and they're tough to keep at a safe temperature so that guests don't get an upset stomach from the first party of the weekend.

We're seeing more of those Edible Arrangements platters served at cocktail parties, giving guests their choice of pull-out fruit kebobs, some of which are dipped in chocolate or cut into the shapes of daisies or other fun party shapes. So think about using this fabulous fruit feature not just as a buffet item but as a centerpiece for the buffet.

Desserts

Even an early afternoon cocktail party benefits from the presence of sweets on the menu, so set out a platter of mini cupcakes in creative flavors such as cotton candy, red velvet, banana split, and carrot cake. A higher-priced dessert feature is a platter of petits fours and easy-to-make chocolate-dipped strawberries.

A cake isn't necessary for this party, since guests will certainly have other wedding cakes to look forward to, and the bride and groom may not want to serve the second rum-flavored cake of the weekend! So it's best to steer clear of cakes—and save a bundle as you do so—choosing finger food desserts instead.

Drinks

An open bar is essential for your party room soirée, since it's a top etiquette rule that guests are never to pay for their own drinks, or tip, during the official hours of any wedding celebration. When you're at a hotel lounge, the open bar tab covers the costs of drinks during the official hours of the party; and when the party ends guests may choose to buy additional drinks or rounds to keep socializing.

Whatever your arrangement—on-site bar or a bar set up in your home—the best drink assortments offer something for everyone. At a lounge, guests can choose from creative cocktails. You can match that offering at your home with an array of tropical cocktails such as Malibu Bay Breezes and rum punches. Martini bars' drink lists are ultra-creative, including even a blue-colored drink called the Fish Bowl with little gummi fish in them. That too can be replicated in your home following a recipe from Cocktail.com and other online sites.

Serve standard and light beers along with an array of microbrew beers, several types of red wine and several types of white wine, fruity drinks served in the form of sangrias or mixer drinks such as cranberry juice with flavored vodka.

Soft drinks can be covered in the form of pitchers of iced teas or sodas.

Money Mastery

Party supply stores have very inexpensive plastic drink pitchers to choose from, and you can keep them for your future parties.

One presentation trend that's finding a place at many welcome cocktail parties is setting a tray of colorful champagne cocktails at the party entrance. When guests arrive, the first thing they see is a party-smart drink awaiting them. That's the kind of impressive detail that makes any style of cocktail party, particularly ones hosted at home, look like a more upscale party.

Planning Details

With your location chosen, your menu ideas and drink offerings in mind, it's time to focus on the additional essentials of planning this type of event.

Invitations

Send out print or Evite invitations to guests far in advance, so that they can make their travel plans to arrive in time for your fun welcome party. Capture the style and formality of your party in your invitation design, such as showing a bubbling glass of champagne for a more formal get-together in the hotel's party room, or a collection of bright cocktails on an illustrated modern invitation to show your at-home cocktail party's style.

Sample wording on your invitation can be: "Please join us upon your arrival at the hotel for a guest welcome party! We'll be in the hotel lounge, so look for us there! The party starts at 4 pm and goes until 6 pm, after which you're free to join friends and family in your own dinner outings."

This wording gives guests the location, the party's timing, and also lets them know that dinner's up to them. You will not be serving a meal.

Money Mastery

Use the fabulous free map-creation website WeddingMapper.com to show where the party will take place. You can print out a map or directions to enclose in printed invitations, or include the map's URL in e-mailed invitations.

Another way to convey this important fact: "Please join us at Bill & Sarah's house for a welcome get-together featuring some delightful wine and hors d'oeuvre pairings."

Again, guests know this is a cocktail party featuring hors d'oeuvres, not a sit-down dinner.

In addition to the all-important indicators about what's on the menu, it's important to provide location information. Don't assume that all guests have booked rooms at the main hotel where the room block is. Some book nearby rooms in a more affordable hotel, some book at bed-and-breakfasts, some stay with relatives. So always provide the name and address of the hotel where the party will take place.

Décor

Unless this is a formal welcome cocktail party, a parents' domain to show off their party-planning prowess and deep pockets, décor doesn't have to be big and impressive. A few small, low-set flower clusters set around the room and placed in several spots on the buffet table is all that's needed. And, of course, classic votive candles are always fantastic décor items found on a budget at a party supply store or craft shop and used to accent the party's color scheme.

In years past, party hosts created banners for the guests' welcome and as a surprise décor treat for the guests of honor. You can have these made at your local sign print shop, in lengths of 4 feet to 8 feet or more, in bright colors with graphics and colorful metallic streamers hanging from the ends.

Another popular décor option is the photo mat set on an entry table with several markers. Guests sign their names and best wishes on the mat surrounding a photo of the bride and groom currently placed within the frame's opening. But party hosts are now replacing that couple portrait with a very fun picture taken at the welcome cocktail party, often a group shot of the couple's circle of friends freshly arrived, excited and ready to celebrate the wedding weekend.

The welcome cocktail party can have its own theme with the décor to match, and it may be chosen by the bride and groom to bring in one of the themes they originally had considered as their reception theme. By allowing their input and planning, say, a *Great Gatsby*-themed party with hosts in 1920s outfits and guests given flapper headbands with feathers, the bride and groom get the Gatsby party décor they had hoped to have as their reception theme.

Along the same lines, the bride and groom may contribute their ideas for décor by telling you about other elements they didn't get into their day. "My groom wanted a basketball-shaped cake for the reception, but that didn't fit with the ultra-formal wedding. So we told our friends about that, and they planned the welcome cocktail party as a surprise theme for my groom! Orange and white colors, a basketball-shaped cake, 'courtside seats' and party favors of little team-icon giveaways. We wore team jerseys and cheerleader outfits, and the party started off the weekend with a ton of fun that the groom especially loved!" —Carla, bridesmaid

Additional Details

Here are some additional ideas to make your welcome cocktail party a hit:

> ➤ Plan the menu to suit the weather. If it's a winter wedding and guests just drove through a snowstorm, serve hot spiked drinks and hot chocolates to warm them up. A hot summer day calls for frozen tropical drinks.

> ➤ Plan this party as the event taking place while the rehearsal dinner is going on. In today's weddings, not all rehearsal dinner hosts can afford to host all out-of-town guests, so your party saves the day by giving them enjoyable appetizers and drinks as a little something to treat arriving guests.

> ➤ If guests arrive after the party ends, arrange to have the leftover bottles of beer and small trays of your party desserts brought up to their hotel rooms. They can't help delayed flights and traffic snarls, so your thoughtful gesture arranged with the hotel manager welcomes them wonderfully, and may also provide them with a note letting them know that your group is still downstairs at the bar.

> ➤ Use fun single-use cameras at this party, setting one on each guest table or just one on the entrance table.

> ➤ Provide easy, free entertainment with your iPod dock, but set it up close to your table so that you can keep an eye on it. Sadly, equipment theft happens at hotel party rooms that can be accessed by strangers, so keep that machine close to you and also place it far from the room entrance doors.

> ➤ If you're the bride and groom hosting this party at your home, use some of your shower gifts, such as entertaining trays, your martini glasses, serving bowls, pitchers, and other items that guests will recognize as what they gave you at the shower. This may be your first big party in your new home, and it's all the more special because it's also the first big get-together of your wedding weekend.

CHAPTER 8

The Rehearsal Dinner and Additional Dinners Out or In

In This Chapter

➤ Rehearsal dinners for the traditionally minded

➤ Rehearsal dinners that show off your creativity

➤ Other special dinners

➤ Tips for dinner planning

After the rehearsal is complete, the bride and groom, their immediate families, the bridal party and their guests, the officiant and guest, and anyone else who's playing a role in the ceremony attend the rehearsal dinner. If you thought I left out "and the fifty out-of-town guests" from that attendee list, you'll be glad to know that rehearsal dinners have for the most part switched back to being events just for the bridal group. It's no longer a must, nor is it realistic, to invite all out-of-town guests to the rehearsal dinner. That practice was a positive one when there were just six or so out-of-town guests traveling in for the wedding, and it was a nice gesture for the bride's family to invite them to dine along with the bride and groom and their inner circle.

Etiquette Friendly

It's good manners to provide out-of-town guests either a cocktail party at which food is served, or a nighttime event at the hotel where wine and light hors d'oeuvres are served. You might also provide your out-of-town guests with a bottle of wine and some edibles in their welcome baskets, so that they may plan their own get-togethers in their hotel rooms.

Now, since we are a global society and wedding couples have an average of forty out-of-town guests, it's just a ridiculous, expensive notion to add that many people to a per-person catered event. So we're back to out-of-towners making their own dinner plans, and then joining the bride and groom at a nighttime cocktail party planned by the wedding couple or by a friend of the family.

That's not all that has changed. Now, rehearsal dinners may be traditional sit-down dinners in a family-style restaurant, themed dinners, or unique interactive dining experiences. This chapter shares some options in planning an unforgettable rehearsal dinner for the bride and groom to share with their inner circle.

Traditional Rehearsal Dinners

The best-known style of rehearsal dinner is one held at a restaurant's or hotel's private party room, with the circle of guests treated to a wonderful sit-down dinner. The dinner is often three courses, including an appetizer, salad course, and entrée, and coffee and dessert are also offered to guests.

While many traditional rehearsal dinner hosts choose exceptional menus for this dinner party, the star is not the food. It's the succession of toasts and presentations started off by the first toast of the evening, proposed by the host. As all guests take their seats, your speech welcomes them to the occasion, sets the tone of the evening with a light and humorous delivery, and wishes the couple a happy life together. A rousing chorus of "Cheers!" and "Hear! Hear!" leads to the clinking of glasses, and the evening proceeds with additional toasts and the presentations of gifts from the wedding couple to the bridal party and parents.

Why Go Traditional

Brides and grooms who choose this long-standing traditional form of rehearsal dinner say that they and their families appreciate having a touch of "the way it's always been done" in the midst of their highly customized creative weddings. They may have given their ceremony personalized twists and themed their reception, and a traditional rehearsal dinner provides the balance of old-world style in their nontraditional wedding plans. "My groom's parents weren't too thrilled about our themed wedding plans, or the fact that we weren't getting married in a church, so it made them feel so much better to have a traditional, semiformal rehearsal dinner that the closest relatives would attend," says Naomi, a recent bride. And Kelly reminds of the obvious, "Hey, his parents are paying for the rehearsal dinner, so if what they really want to do is a traditional rehearsal dinner, we're okay with that. It's better than if they wanted to do a really out-there theme party like some of my friends' parents have done!"

Three Styles of Traditional When Dining Out

The restaurant you choose as the location for the traditional rehearsal dinner is sure to have a special event menu for you to peruse. Upon this planning meeting, you'll decide which of the three main styles of traditional rehearsal dinners you'll arrange.

> ➤ Prix fixe rehearsal dinners: The restaurant will show you its list of catering choices for your review. Most hosts show this list to the bride and groom for their input on courses selected from the list of offerings. After all, the bride and groom know what's on the menus for their cocktail party and reception, and you never want to duplicate any dish they're serving at their wedding. So it's a must to get clearance on that chicken piccata. You'll choose an appetizer, a salad, and two or three entrée options to present to guests, then a dessert to be served to all. The package comes at a per-person cost, and virtually all restaurants will be able to customize dishes for your special dietary requests such as gluten free and no pork.

> ➤ À la carte rehearsal dinners: For this style of dinner, guests are free to order whatever they'd like off the regular menu. There's no preselected appetizer or trio of entrée choices on a set party menu. With a smaller group invited to this traditional dinner, many hosts simply let their closest friends and family members choose what they'd like for their meals and desserts.

> ➤ Buffet rehearsal dinners: Some restaurants are known for their amazing, impressive buffet dinners, and it's become a budget-friendly, indulgent trend to host a traditional rehearsal dinner at an established buffet. Many hosts say that a restaurant's or hotel's brunch offers a variety of hot and cold gourmet platters that they'd never be able to self-cater, and the dessert bar is also a winning proposition for their guests.

Money Mastery

Forget about the stigma of the early bird seating. It's just smart to spend $10 less per person at a 6 pm dinner seating time, especially when you're paying for a big group. Speak with the bride and groom about coordinating an early time for their rehearsal so that your group can be seated at the earlier, less expensive, hours to enjoy the same gourmet foods those 9 pm patrons are spending a lot more to enjoy!

Another money-saving secret: if you host the rehearsal dinner at the same hotel where the wedding will be taking place, where the guests are staying, and where the morning-after breakfast is booked, you may be granted a sizeable discount on this event by the hotel's special events manager. Hotels love to reward loyal customers with budget-saving breaks and freebies, and some rehearsal dinner hosts say that the hotel's events manager threw in a cake and dessert coffees for free, or upgraded to premium liquors at their open bar while charging them for house brands. It's something to keep in mind when you're considering where to host your chosen style of rehearsal dinner.

At-Home Traditional

Another possibility is hosting the rehearsal dinner at your home, either setting your dining room table with your good china and crystal stemware for a family-style sit-down dinner, or setting up a dinner buffet for your guests to enjoy. Some hosts hire caterers to prepare and serve the food in their home, cutting down their workload and allowing them to enjoy the party, and others relish the opportunity to entertain in true family holiday style.

As the host and perhaps as the chef, you can arrange for a several-course meal featuring your own family-favorite recipes as a special treat for the bride and groom who love your chicken cacciatore or your beef bourguignon. This at-home, family-centric meal becomes a wonderful gift to the couple, and gathers the family together in a warm and cozy setting.

Steal My Party Idea

"We had a caterer deliver hot trays of entrées and appetizers, set them up for us on Sterno-heated stands, and we had no food prep to worry about!"– Melissa, bride

An at-home rehearsal dinner in any meal style, sit-down or buffet, provides you with the freedom to have your party last as long as you wish, and you get complete privacy for those all-important toasts and gift exchanges. An interesting dimension of the at-home party is that guests feel more comfortable departing after the meal and dessert than they would at a restaurant event where it would be rude to get up and leave before the check arrives. At this laid-back event, parents and grandparents might depart after the official rehearsal dinner event, while the bride and groom remain at your place with their close friends to enjoy after-dinner drinks and some quality shared time. A restaurant will likely frown upon your group remaining at a table after your dinner is complete, since they want to seat the next group of patrons.

Creative Rehearsal Dinners

In today's world of creative wedding plans, it's become a fun new trend to get creative with the rehearsal dinner as well. Parents who are planning this dinner, or the wedding couple if they are the hosts, now embrace the opportunity to give this dinner a twist. Here are the top trends in creative rehearsal dinners.

Theme Dinners

If a theme did not work for the wedding reception, it may be used for the rehearsal dinner. It could be a sports theme, with guests invited to wear their favorite team jerseys or team logo T-shirts and with a sports-themed cake on the menu. It could be a Mardi Gras theme, with colorful beads playing a large factor in the dinner décor. It could be a Hawaiian luau hosted in the parents' backyard, complete with a tiki bar and coconuts and pineapples as table centerpieces. A popular trend right now is the black-and-white-themed rehearsal dinner, with guests invited to wear black and/or white outfits, and the décor planned in all black and white, even the cake is iced in a black-and-white pattern.

Another popular trend in theme dinners is basing the menu and décor on the couple's heritage, such as a Thai dinner or a Slavic dinner or a Japanese dinner—whatever their bloodline may be. Within this theme are countless opportunities for décor and good luck symbols from the particular culture, such as a Korean symbol of a pair of doves said to mate for life.

The menu consists of traditional cultural foods, in authentic form, prepared by family elders—a real treat for the bride and groom who might not have tasted a grandmother's lasagna or pierogies in ages. Desserts, too, bring a culture's sweet and symbolic offerings, such as good fortune, prosperity, and happiness, to the couple's celebration as they did to generations of family ancestors at their weddings. Add in décor based in the culture's signature colors and favors inspired by cultural tastes or the arts, and your performance as a party host will be quite appreciated and admired by all.

Of course, the theme and cuisine need not match the bride's or groom's own cultural backgrounds but may simply reflect a culture loved by the bride and groom. It may be a so-called adventurous theme with Moroccan or Thai cuisine. Perhaps the wedding's region is known for having an amazing local cuisine, such as Chicago deep-dish pizza, and the couple wants to treat their closest guests to an authentic regional dish and the theme to go with it. Ask the bride and groom if they'd like their rehearsal dinner based in any type of cultural or regional tastes to help you plan this all-important dinner for them and their closest guests.

Interactive Restaurants

Some nontraditional couples take unique dining a step further, going beyond cultural dining or a theme party to the unique experience of an interactive restaurant. Think about the performance at a hibachi restaurant, where the skilled chef flips tiny bits of zucchini for guests to catch in their mouths, or the pizza place where the chef comes out into the dining room to show off his dough-twirling skills.

Steal My Party Idea

"For our rehearsal dinner, we took everyone to one of those murder mystery dinner places, where actors join in with the guests, everyone's given a role to play, and everyone has to solve the murder of the evening. It was a riot to see some of our shy friends get into the acting, flirting with the actors, and also to see the parents having a fun time playing along!"—Mandy and Tom, newlyweds

Steal My Party Idea

"We knew the bride was so upset over not being able to have a cake from the celebrity baker she always dreamed about for her wedding cake. The reception hall wouldn't allow any outside catering or bakers' works. So we got her the Cake Boss cake for her rehearsal dinner as a surprise!"—Stephanie, bridesmaid

Think about performance dining such as dinner theaters. Try a country western restaurant where the waiters sing and dance choreographed numbers in the aisles, and line dances take place on the dance floor for guests to participate in.

Interactive may also mean the scenery around the party, which may change when you're on a dinner cruise, passing by breathtaking scenery on an island or in a city's harbor.

The Bride's and Groom's Rescued Inspirations

You can rescue the bride and groom's original wedding wishes, those elements or themes they wanted for their wedding reception but were outvoted or didn't have the budget to undertake. When you open the topic with the bride and groom, you may be able to plan the outdoor dinner they originally had hoped for (but was quashed due to the logistics of moving two hundred people indoors), or the clambake they couldn't afford for two hundred guests (but you can afford for twenty), or the theme that the bride's cousin just had at her wedding three months ago and cannot be used again in front of the same relatives attending this wedding (but it's okay at the rehearsal dinner!).

Additional Dinners

The rehearsal dinner is not the only special dinner possible during the wedding weekend. When guests are in town for several days—or when everyone's attending a destination wedding that lasts the span of four or five days to make the flight there worth it—opportunities for festive dinner parties abound.

Before the Wedding

Bridal party members and their guests, as well as relatives and friends from far away, may decide to arrive in town a few days before the wedding both to be present for pre-wedding essentials (the bridal party) and to have time to visit with local relatives and friends (additional guests). These out-of-towners may take advantage of better-priced airfare on a Wednesday and arrive in town before everyone else arrives on Friday.

The trends now for these pre-wedding dinner parties include the following:

➤ The bride and groom plan a dinner for their bridal party members and their guests, just to have quiet, private time to share with them, give them their gifts, and thank them for their help as they planned the wedding. This dinner might be a casual one, or the couple may wish to splurge, taking this small circle to a fine dining establishment.

➤ The bride and groom plan a dinner for a select group of long-distance friends who they rarely get to see. Before the craziness of the wedding's forty-eight hours, this is the perfect chance to go to a restaurant with friends from college who haven't reunited in five or more years, plus all of their kids who most of the group haven't met yet.

➤ Parents plan a dinner event for their in-town relatives and longtime best friends, again either going casual or splurging on a five-star dinner.

➤ Wedding guests plan their own dinner events, without the bride and groom or their family, to give themselves time to visit with their own relatives—perhaps from the other side of the family—or friends, or to attend a special event in the area. They may treat themselves to theater tickets in the nearby city, with dinner at a famous restaurant as their vacation's other highlight.

Post-Wedding

The same groups may plan dinners with friends or family scheduled for the night after the wedding. When most others have left town after the morning-after breakfast, these groups remain at the hotel or stay at a relative's or friend's house, or venture to a nearby resort town to continue their visits with local loved ones.

In busy wedding season, which now encompasses May through October, the day after the wedding may be spoken for. It might be the day of another friend's or relative's bridal or baby shower, an anniversary party, or a graduation party. With all of the relatives already taking the trip into town for the wedding, relatives may schedule their own special event for after the wedding, ensuring that far-away relatives can attend while only having to make one cross-country flight that summer. It's not encroaching on the wedding, since the wedding is officially over. With the hosts of those parties perhaps booking the afternoon hours to plan a lunch, barbecue, or cocktail party, the guests' evening is now open for a potential dinner plan.

And, of course, a trendy Friday night wedding may lead to a Saturday night dinner shared with friends. These dinners are now hot events since many of us live so far from friends that we relish the chance to socialize with them on the rare occasions that bring everyone into the same town. Some brides and grooms even delay their honeymoon departure dates by a few days so that they can be present for the post-wedding dinners planned by their friends. Some brides and grooms dip into their wedding gift money to host an all-inclusive dinner so that they can see everyone at one event, rather than divide their time between two separate events planned by his friends and her friends.

Planning Tips

With your party's style and location decided, it's time to delve into the planning details that make your rehearsal dinner a stylish success.

Invitations

Rehearsal dinner invitations conform to the same invitation etiquette rules as wedding invitations when it comes to addressing them. When a couple is invited to the rehearsal dinner, you send the invitation to "Mr. and Mrs. Jeffrey Smith." If your event will be less formal, it's perfectly okay to address the invitation to "Jeffrey and Sarah Smith." If the Smiths' kids are invited, the envelope will be written as follows:

Jeffrey and Sarah Smith and Family

Or

Jeffrey and Sarah Smith
Emily Smith
Ashley Smith

That covers the etiquette for the printed and mailed invitation addressing. If you choose to send an Evite or other e-mailed invitation—as is perfectly okay for rehearsal dinner invitation etiquette—you'll send the e-invite to the recipient's e-mail address, and then write a personal note in the message box explaining who exactly is on the guest list. You might write, "We're hoping that you, Jeff, Emily, and Ashley can join us!" It's crucially important to invite people specifically so that you don't run into the headache of receiving RSVPs for four when two were invited to your adults-only dinner.

Etiquette aside, the design of your invitations reflects the style and theme of the dinner, and the most popular invitation graphics include wine glasses, floral centerpieces, and a colorful table setting closeup featuring a gorgeous china plate and a cobalt blue charger with stemware reflecting candlelight—the idyllic formal table setting.

Etiquette Friendly

Single guests invited to the rehearsal are most often allowed to bring a guest with them, so that guest would properly be invited to the rehearsal dinner as well. As an important first step, speak with the bride about whether she is offering her single bridesmaids and ceremony participants the option of bringing a guest. She and the groom might not want a huge crowd of dates and noisy onlookers at the rehearsal, in which case they'd want you to invite their single friends without a plus one to the rehearsal dinner. The bride and groom always get to decide who's included, and as host you need to get their specific instructions before sending out an invitation and potentially causing a diplomatic problem for them.

Another top trend in rehearsal dinner invitations is simply choosing a color scheme for an elegantly simple single-panel invitation in a pretty hue such as sage green or tan or lavender with a darker color decorative font spelling out the party details.

Rehearsal dinner hosts find it most fitting both creatively and budget-wise to make their own invitations using their computer's design software or an invitation-making program like that in the Martha Stewart collection or the inexpensive invitation software from Mountaincow.com. With pretty invitation cards purchased at the craft store, you can design your own custom invitations, add borders and small, subtle graphics, and even place the couple's decorative monogram on the top of the card.

Hole punches and pattern-edged craft scissors allow you to create a cutout or scalloped pattern along an edge of the invitation, and design experts advise you to keep your cutouts to one edge of the invitation only for the most upscale look. A card that's been scallop cut on all sides tends to look like a child's school project, going just a touch too far with the creativity. Less is always more when it comes to DIY accents to invitations.

Shop Here!

If you'd like to design and order custom-printed invitations rather than make them, but you think that you'd have to place an order for way more printed invitations than you need, Vistaprint.com now offers a pretty range of invitations in packs of ten or twenty, the perfect number for your small party. And I've seen—and have purchased—invitation packs for between $7 and $15.

To avoid confusing out-of-town guests who assume they'll be invited to the rehearsal dinner, it's best for the bride and groom to keep all mention of rehearsal and rehearsal dinner plans off of their personal wedding website. Invitations sent via print or e-mail contain all of the information guests need about location, including the site's full address to enter into a GPS or driving direction printouts courtesy of the free mapping site WeddingMapper.com. When out-of-town guests don't get an invitation to the rehearsal dinner within weeks of the wedding, they understand that this is one of those events they're not invited to. And most guests fully understand that it's all about budget, nothing personal.

Décor

A rehearsal dinner hosted at a hotel's ballroom opens the opportunity for you to select table linens and place setting styles through the special events office when you book your event. And it's then up to you to contact a floral designer, if you wish, to arrange for expertly created floral centerpieces. Or, you may wish to create budget-friendly DIY low-set floral centerpieces for each table. You might make your own floral bunch centerpieces in little glass vases, or skip the flowers in favor of colorful pillar, taper, or votive candles, which you can surround with color-matched flower petals as a lovely and inexpensive centerpiece design. A single glass round bowl with a floating flower in it costs less than $10 per table, a smart idea for a classy, subtle centerpiece.

Money Mastery

At a restaurant-set rehearsal dinner, you might not need any décor at all, since the restaurant itself may routinely set their guest tables with pretty candles and fresh flower bunches.

For your at-home tables, the same type of small floral centerpieces work well, and framed family photos may be put on display for this party, as they have been at wedding receptions for years. It's a new trend to display precious family photos at the rehearsal dinner, keeping them safe at home and not risking any damage to them in transport to the reception site. It also adds a wonderful sentimentality to an at-home rehearsal dinner.

Entertainment

The restaurant may have on-site entertainment providing musical ambiance for your event, and some live performances truly bring down the house, even providing the chance for the bride and groom to stand up and slow dance. Restaurants often have the ability to pipe music into their private party rooms, so that your group can enjoy the performance by the jazz group, guitarist, pianist, or band playing in the main dining room. That makes your exciting entertainment feature free to you.

If you'll be providing your own soundtrack, it's a wonderful idea to ask a music-savvy friend to create a theme-matched playlist for the party. A friend who asks if there is anything she can do to help will delight in getting to participate by compiling fabulous songs for the rehearsal dinner's hours. And the couple's kids may even be the music masters for this party. Kids and teens love participating and receiving applause from party guests when it's revealed that they designed the iPod soundtrack.

Toasts

The highlight of any rehearsal dinner is the words spoken at it, the toasts to the bride and groom and their future happiness. As mentioned earlier, you—as the host—are the first to propose a toast to the happy couple. At this relaxed and enjoyable dinner, a brief and humor-tinged toast is a delightful way to begin the festivities. Start by introducing yourself, since there may be relatives and friends in the room who do not know who you are—if you are not the bride or groom, naturally—and share a fun anecdote about your relationship with the bride or groom or both. For instance, "I've known Shelly for over fifteen years, starting from our first day in junior high when she was the only person to talk to the shy new kid." That story pays tribute to the bride's kind nature.

Steal My Party Idea

"We decided to share our something old, something new, something borrowed, and something blue rituals with our rehearsal dinner guests. I held up my departed grandmother's own wedding day necklace, which my mother had given me to wear for my wedding, and our relatives loved seeing that. My groom presented me with my something new, a pair of diamond earrings that were his gift to me. My sister gave me her beaded wedding purse that she carried at her wedding, my something borrowed. And the groom's sister gave us a Tiffany blue box with a keychain as a gift from their side of the family, that we'd use for the keys to our future home. I couldn't have dreamed of a better celebration of us all becoming a happy extended family."—Kimberly, bride

The next phase of a wonderful toast addresses the bride and groom's relationship, how you knew the bride had found The One when she stopped wearing ponytails and sweats to class and started borrowing your clothes. Again, guests will love getting that inside look at the beginning of the couple's courtship. You can talk about how impressed you and your circle of friends or family were at the groom's generous nature, how he helped paint your house after knowing the bride for just a few weeks, how he brought over sandwiches for the family after the loss of a relative. There's a nod to the groom's comforting nature and generosity of spirit.

You'll then wish them every happiness and a life filled with every dream come true, and you'll speak directly to the groom or the bride, welcoming them into the family. You've just proposed a fabulous toast to start the evening's parade of toasts. Next up may be the bride and groom toasting you and their guests and parents for helping to plan the wedding. And parents, too, love to welcome their new son- or daughter-in-law into the family with a sweet and touching toast that's followed by hugs and handshakes.

The bride and groom may then wish to give out gifts to their families and to their bridal party members, although some couples now choose to give out presents at the wedding morning breakfast instead of before a crowd of guests who may not be receiving gifts. That is the personal decision of the bride and groom.

CHAPTER 9

The After-Party

> **In This Chapter**
>
> ➤ Choosing your party's style
>
> ➤ What to serve
>
> ➤ Tips on planning your after-party

The celebration doesn't have to stop when the lights come on, the music ends, and the reception is over. Now, it's a big trend—very nearly a must—for the festivities to continue after the reception's closing notes. This chapter will provide the top styles of after-parties and will help you design the after-party you may choose to host. Will you plan ahead for a separate catered event in a hotel's smaller party room as some big-budget hosts do? Or will you invite guests to join the group at the hotel bar immediately following the reception's end? As host, you get to choose, of course with input from the bride and groom.

And speaking of hosts, keep in mind that *anyone* can host an after-party. The bride and groom can invite their closest friends to a post-party event, parents especially love to invite their own friends and close relatives to their own private after-party, and since some brides and grooms have multiple sets of parents, it's now a trend for this party to be hosted by a parental set who didn't get to host the rehearsal dinner or the morning-after breakfast. Parents want to plan and share the fun, so this is one area that's gaining a lot of momentum for the parent-hosted soirée.

Read on to explore party styles by location, as well as the top trends in menu selections, invitation styles, and many other guest-thrilling details of this wedding weekend event.

Setting Your Style

First, you'll need to choose your party's style, and that style—and its full range of details—will always depend on the time when the reception ends. Many budget-conscious brides and grooms are holding afternoon weddings that begin at noon and end at 5 pm, so an after-party that begins at 5 pm will have to offer a menu that counts as a dinner. For a wedding that begins at 3 pm and ends at 9 pm, the after-party is prime for a cocktail party event, with drinks and both light and heavy hors d'oeuvres on the menu. For a formal wedding that begins at 8 pm and ends at 1 am, your late-night after-party may be a cocktail party, but some groups opt to change into comfy clothes and go to a diner for fries and burgers like they used to when they were in school. A variety of after-party styles are available for you to explore once you know the start time of your event.

Spontaneous Hotel Gathering

As the most common after-party style, close friends of the bride and groom simply follow them out the ballroom doors and to the hotel's lounge, where you'll get a few tables and attract plenty of attention for being in your wedding wardrobes. Party hosts say that the hotel bar manager will often provide the bride and groom with a complimentary cocktail, or bring a bottle of champagne over to your table for your group to enjoy.

Steal My Party Idea

"We were going to host the after-party up in our hotel room, but when we saw the hotel lounge's amazing list of martini flavors and saw that it had a raw bar right there, we changed the setting to the very cool hotel lounge—which turned out to be genius, since we found out the hotel had a policy of forbidding guests to bring in their own liquor supplies to the hotel! Had we bought cases of wine and beer for our hotel room, we would have been stopped by hotel security and forced to put the liquor back out into the car!"–Christine, bridesmaid

If you like the ease of this party style, check out the hotel's lounge ahead of time to see if it's nice enough to be the setting of your get-together. Some hotel lounges are very upscale, with modern décor, fabulous lighting, and top-of-the-line bar menus. Other lounges can be a bit less impressive. It all depends on the hotel the bride and groom have chosen for their wedding location. As host, it's your party's success on the line, so be sure to pop into the lounge for a quick look around and a glance at its bar menu.

The spontaneous hotel bar gathering does present a few challenges. Keeping your guest list small, including just the bride and groom's closest friends, will be a little tough, since other out-of-town wedding guests staying in the hotel will probably head right to the hotel lounge as well. And when they see your group in a corner booth, they are likely to just walk over and join you. It's not party crashing; it's just a natural move, since—as many wedding guests say—they don't want to seem rude by sitting a few tables away and not joining the toasts to the bride and groom.

Etiquette Friendly

It's perfectly okay for you to use the same type of payment arrangement that you use when you go out to a bar or lounge with your circle of friends. If the one who plans the outing always picks up the tab, that's your group's accepted payment etiquette. If you always split the tab, that's your plan. But you must tell friends that this will be the plan at this after-party. Just say, "Hey, we're all going to the hotel lounge now to continue the party. Are you okay with splitting the tab? There's an ATM in the lobby, and I'm headed there now." Guests can decide if they want to join you or not. But you've been clear about it. That's one acceptable plan if you have that kind of relationship with the close friends/guests. Many brides and grooms would be mad if you told guests you don't know that they have to split the tab. So talk with the bride and groom first to see if they're okay with your plan to have everyone share the bill. They might be embarrassed, which is the opposite of what etiquette is designed to achieve. It's also etiquette friendly for the first round or two to be on you, and then you close out the tab on your own, letting guests know that it's now a pay-per-drink party. They'll be having a great time and may not mind. Plus, ending the party after an hour lets the bride and groom depart for their alone time.

So if your out-of-town guests are the bride and groom's close circle of friends, and if the elders are going to the parents' after-party, you might not have a problem at all!

The other concern is the bar tab. As host, it's most often essential for you to pick up the tab for your group's after-party at the hotel lounge. That's why this type of after-party is very often hosted by the entire bridal party, who have made prearrangements to split the tab for this gathering. Many brides and grooms, a little buzzed on their reception drinks, have been known to plunk down their credit cards to cover the costs of this after-party with their friends. So the issue is raised: what's the etiquette for paying for this type of party?

Another element of the after-party held at the hotel lounge is that you might choose to order several platters of appetizers for your group to share. It might be hours after dinner was served at the reception, so you'd be a wonderful host to provide some chicken fingers, spinach and artichoke dip with chips, cheese straws, and other easy-to-share bites for your guests. So do expect the addition of some menu items in the cost of this type of party.

Booking a Room

Some styles of after-parties are nicer than many birthday parties out there! For this type of party, hosts book a small party room in the hotel or in a nearby restaurant, banquet tables are set with pretty tablecloths and floral or candle centerpieces, as well as new single-use cameras, a bar is set in the corner of the room, and a deejay plays for guests to continue dancing into the late-night hours. In many ways, this style of after-party resembles a small wedding. Some hosts go all out, hiring lighting designers, commissioning ice sculptures, and getting photo booths for guests to enjoy.

Your party room party doesn't have to include all of these upscale elements. Just the booked party room, catering, bar, décor, and entertainment are the norm. Again, it's like a small wedding or a milestone birthday or anniversary party.

A fabulous trend is making this a themed party. Brides and grooms say they love having the chance to experience a particular theme that they may have wanted for their reception, but ultimately decided not to do, whether for budget reasons or family opinions. "We really wanted to do a Mardi Gras-themed wedding, but my groom's parents were really against it and actually threatened to take away their funding of the wedding if we did do it. So we were disappointed to lose that dream of ours, until my bridesmaids offered to plan a Mardi Grasthemed after-party! We had our beads, our brightly colored décor with masks and feathers, beignets, hurricanes, jazz music—all for our *friends* at the party! It was fabulous!" says Jennifer, a recent bride.

For this formal style of party, themed or not, guests arrive in their wedding clothes, and the bride and groom wear their wedding finery. Many brides choose to change into their second dress for this event. It's become a trend for brides to wear a formal wedding gown for the reception, and then change into a different style of dress, perhaps a sheath or a cocktail-length dress, for their after-party. And for a theme party, the couple might change into costumes and provide costume props for guests to wear or carry, which provides for fantastic photo ops.

At-Home Party

For a more relaxed style, you might choose to host the after-party in your home. With a buffet of light appetizers set up on the dining room table or side table, guests happily remove their high heels and take their places on couches and comfy chairs, glasses of wine or champagne in hand, to enjoy an evening of mingling and reminiscing about the day.

A party held at home allows you to extend the party for as long as you wish. You're not limited by an end time, as you would be at a hotel party room or lounge. And your home provides privacy for your party, containing the guest list to just the people you invite to join you.

If you have a lovely outdoor terrace, and weather permits, decorate it with strings of lights and have your party in the open air. If you have a pool and hot tub, guests may love the chance to take a dip.

Outdoor Adventure

The outdoor adventure is especially attractive for destination weddings and wedding locales near a beach or lake. After the reception ends, say, at an island resort, everyone takes their champagne glasses out to the beach to sit on lounge chairs or view the sunrise—or sunset, as the case may be—over the ocean. At an island resort, you do need to mind your noise level so as not to disturb other resort guests, so talk to your events manager about designating an area for your after-party. Many will clear an area for you, marked off with tiki torches to add extra exotic ambience. Or they'll set up a bar and buffet on a private beach area you can call your own for this after-party in paradise.

Steal My Party Idea

"We loaded our digital camera memory cards into our home theater systems and played a slideshow of photos taken during the wedding day to give guests—including the bride and groom—an exciting showing of the wonderful images from the wedding day and reception."— Diane, mother of the bride

Watch Out!

Be mindful of the feelings of guests who aren't invited to your after-party. I heard about a disaster at the close of a wedding reception: the bride and groom arranged for signs outside the hotel, instructing guests of the after-party to wait in a section marked off by a velvet rope, while the uninvited stood in line for the valets to bring them their cars. Feelings were very hurt by this visible display of in group and out group, most of whom asked what was going on and found out that the VIP guests were headed out to a champagne dinner cruise hosted by the bride and groom. Ouch! To avoid this nightmare, tell your invited after-party guests to meet at a designated area of the hotel lobby at least a half hour after the close of the reception. That also gives them time to go to their rooms and freshen up before the next party commences.

Let's Go Out

For a party out on the town, the bride and groom and their VIP guests take the hotel shuttle to a piano bar, jazz bar, dance club, or even a diner or fast food place for their after-party. Talk with the hotel manager to see if the wedding group can use its free shuttle for this outing, or if you can pay to rent the shuttle for the evening, providing all with a safe and worry-free ride and perhaps the chance to go clubhopping for the rest of the evening before returning everyone safely to the hotel.

Food and Drinks

As mentioned earlier, the timing of some parties requires that you serve menu items suitable for a dinner hour—including chafing dish entrees and heavy hors d'oeuvres—while some invite cocktail party platters, and some are perfect for late-night bites such as sliders and other bar food items. At an elegant after-party, you might serve an array of desserts and champagne. This section will inspire a menu creation tailored to your after-party style.

Steal My Party Idea

"For our casual at-home party, we just ordered pizzas to be delivered, along with some salads and mozzarella sticks. It was fast, easy, and guests loved having a salad to eat in addition to our veggie, pepperoni, and plain cheese pizzas!"—Claire, bride

Think first about the workload involved in your party's menu. If you'll host an at-home event, the preparation and serving of food will be up to you. So as guests arrive, you'll be in the kitchen heating up platters of food, carrying trays out to the table—working. At one of my own at-home parties, a bit of sauce from a tray I was heating up spilled onto my oven's floor, and my house filled with smoke! So I decided to stick to baking trays of appetizers and cold platters in the future. Prep work after a full wedding day and reception can be exhausting, so if you will be hosting an at-home party, choose trays of menu items that are easy to set out.

On the Menu

Here are a few menu ideas to suit several different types and timings of parties:

➤ Dinner hour parties: Chafing dishes of beef medallions, lemon chicken bites, pasta primavera, mini crab cakes, mini meatballs, along with platters of cocktail party appetizers such spinach puffs, hummus and pita bread triangles, guacamole and chips, and other party platters mentioned in the next section.

➤ Cocktail parties: Buffet platters of shrimp cocktail, baked brie with cranberry sauce inside, roasted red pepper hummus and chips or pita triangles, cheese platter, fresh veggie platter, cheese puffs, pigs in a blanket, sliders, snack mixes, mini sandwich platters (bought at a supermarket or warehouse store like Costco, Sam's Club or BJ's Wholesale), and gourmet chips and dip.

➤ Late-night bites: Cones of French fries, sliders, hot dogs, hot pretzels with cheese dip, pigs in a blanket, and knishes. If your party is super-late, starting at 1 am, you might wish to create a breakfast bar filled with mini bagels and spreads, muffins, crispy bacon, fruit cups, and more.

➤ Dessert hour: In the later hours, post 8 pm, your party will please the sweet tooth with an array of desserts, including little cups of chocolate mousse, gourmet brownies, tiny vanilla tarts with fresh fruit on top, cupcakes, cake balls (a big trend: round balls of cake, fully frosted, and served on a stick), truffles, and fruit platters. The ice cream bar might seem like a good idea, but ice cream melts quickly and can be an uninviting hassle after just a short time. Some guests solve this dilemma by producing boxes of frozen ice pops, ice cream bars, and ice cream sandwiches from their freezer for guests to enjoy, especially at outdoor poolside parties.

Watch Out!

Remember that guests have been drinking for hours before getting to your party, and will continue drinking during your party, so don't tempt disaster by serving foods that can turn stomachs. That crispy bacon or bacon-wrapped scallops or anything fried and greasy are the biggest culprits here. And guests say that after a day filled with so many different kinds of foods, flavors, spices, and sauces, they really enjoy lighter fare at an after-party. Fruit platters are their number one preference for fresh, hydrating snacks.

At the Bar

At the hotel lounge, you might just order several bottles of wine for the table, and guests can order (and pay for) mixed drinks at the bar. At a bar or party room event, you might arrange for an open bar—never a cash bar!—with a selection of wines, beers, and a set number of mixed drinks on the menu. When you limit the types of drinks served and eliminate shots, you keep your bar tab on the more affordable side, and guests still get to choose from a selection of drinks they enjoy.

Since guests have enjoyed drinks at the reception, they will almost certainly appreciate the availability of thirst-quenching soft drinks such as seltzers with lemon or lime, and pitchers of iced tea. And many guests choose the comforting taste of ginger ale as well as the cool, clean refreshment of a glass of spring water. So provide plenty of nonalcoholic options as well.

At a themed party, serve drinks that suit the theme such as brightly colored hurricanes for that Mardi Gras party, tropical piña coladas for your Hawaiian-themed party, Manhattans or sidecars for your 50s-themed party, and more. Check Cocktail.com and FoodNetwork.com to get great cocktail drink recipes, and ask a friend to act as bartender for your at-home or hotel suite party.

Money Mastery

There's no rule saying you have to serve champagne at your after-party, unless you're planning a champagne and dessert party.

A big trend right now is retro drinks, such as those 1950s-era cocktails, as well as fruity punches. That's right—get out or borrow a punch bowl and its matching ladle, and treat guests to a frothy, fruity punch, or an elegant peach and champagne punch with scoops of sorbet melting on top and an ice ring with pieces of fresh fruit frozen inside of it.

As host of an at-home party, you can show your creative style by setting out colorful drink stirrers with your party supply store stock of colorful drink cups and martini glasses, and colored paper napkins. Get a glass-rimming kit and rim your drink glasses with bright pink sugar to match your party's color scheme, and, of course, a glass-rimming kit is essential for rimming a glass with salt if you'll be serving margaritas. Accessorize your drink menu with these fun and inexpensive touches, and your guests will be impressed.

Coffees and Teas

The close of any evening calls for a great cup of coffee in all kinds of flavors. For your after-party, you can serve regular or decaf, or you can offer your guests sweeter flavors such as hazelnut or French vanilla. I'm also a fan of the amazing imported coffee blends and flavors found at Starbucks, adding an exotic flair to my parties when I set out a sign saying this coffee is a fair trade coffee from Namibia.

Also in the coffee realm are the liquored-up favorites: Irish coffee and Jamaican coffee, as well as coffee add-ins like Kahlua and Baileys Irish Cream. You can find recipes for additional booze coffees at Cocktail.com and FoodNetwork.com, as well as at AllRecipes.com and MixingBowl.com.

Tea is a hot property at after-parties as well, with vanilla chai tea leading the pack in creamy flavors, and green tea in several fruit flavors from pomegranate to peach to blueberry to raspberry being also in demand.

To make tea service easier, set out a hot water kettle or dispenser with a sectioned serving tray specifically designed to hold a dozen or more different types of tea bags. Guests then choose their own and customize their tea—or coffee—from your bar of raw sugar, stevia packets, agave nectar, sugar cubes, half-and-half, soy milk, and regular milk. Again, it's these little, additional details that make your coffee and tea bar stand out.

Dessert Drinks

Serve sweet dessert wine with your evening's dessert assortment, and visit WineSpectator.com and FoodandWine.com to learn more about Australian "stickies," which are regional dessert wines. Those sites will also inform you of the newest and award-winning wine pairings for your different desserts—chocolates, creamy desserts, fruity desserts, and more.

Shop Here!

I'm a huge fan of Harney & Sons teas (Harney.com), where you'll find the standards, oolong, black tea, and Earl Grey, in addition to exotic jasmine blends, mango fruit tea, orange passion tea, kiwi-strawberry, Chinese passion tea, cinnamon sunset tea, hot currant, cherry blossom, and more exciting and exotic teas to serve in its signature silk tea bags that impresses guests no end.

And, of course, there are the classic after-dinner drinks such as brandy and cognac that your guests can pour for their late-night indulgence.

Planning Tips

You have lots of inspiration already, so continue on to work through the essential planning steps and style elements.

Your Guest List

Before you book a room or plan a menu, you'll need to know just how big a party this is going to be. If you're not the bride and groom, and if your party includes them—as opposed to a parents' party including just their friends—you'll need to create your guest list with the bride and groom's input. They'll tell you which out-of-town friends to invite so their entire group can be together. A quality VIP guest list that doesn't ruffle any feathers includes all of the members of an established group, and you don't want to cause friction for the bride and groom by leaving someone off the list or by including a person they don't want there, since five more people connected to them would have to come too.

The average after-party guest list includes the bridal party members and their guests, siblings and their guests (if not in the bridal party), close friends from both in and out of town, and close relatives such as cousins. Parents often invite their friends, siblings, parents, close relatives, and relatives from out of town to their parties. What you don't want is a copy of the entire wedding guest list. Just twenty or so people is the norm. If the bridal party is big, eight or more people plus their guests, then that number swells to thirty or forty, which is a lot of people to host in your home or at a lounge.

Etiquette Friendly

What about guests with kids? If the guests' kids are invited to the reception, how do you tell the guests that kids aren't invited to the after-party? You do it directly. "(Name,) I understand that little Billy and little Cassie are invited to the reception, and you're on the invite list for the after-party. What are your plans for the kids, since there are no kids allowed in the bar we're going to after the reception?" That puts some parents in a pickle, and some may tell you they're bringing the kids along, since they have no one to leave them with. That's when you alert the bride and groom to the kiddie dilemma and ask them how they'd like you to handle this situation. Brides and grooms never want you fighting with their relatives or friends, so it's a smart move to bring this issue to their attention, so that they can potentially arrange for a late-night teen babysitter team to watch the kiddies while the parents play.

Invitations

Your invitations can be print, Evites, or other type of online invitation. Evite and Pingg have great cocktail-themed invitations, and I love these graphics for showing a nighttime party: a half moon, dressed-up club goers in brightly hued outfits (to show guests you're going clubbing), and a clock with the hands set at midnight.

A theme party calls for Mardi Gras masks for your New Orleans party, hula dancers or a palm tree for your Hawaiian party, a champagne bottle and glasses for your champagne and desserts party, grapes and cheese platter for your cocktail party, colorful fish or a beach ball for your pool party, and retro diner icons like a neon sign and a 1950s convertible to tell guests you're all going to Johnny Rockets after the reception.

Send your invitations as soon as possible so that guests can make their travel arrangements, and even bring along a babysitter so guests with children can join their circle of friends at this late-night party.

And, yes, some brides and grooms—excitedly and in the moment—do simply extend verbal invitations while at their reception, asking friends to join them at the hotel lounge for a round of drinks on them as a last-minute, spontaneous after-party. No printed invitation needed.

At-Home Party Preps

If you'll be hosting the after-party at your home, you have some extra work to do in super-cleaning your home and setting up for the party the day before the wedding day. Sandwich platters and catering trays need to be picked up the day before the party, or if a roommate can get them the same day, that would be phenomenal, for fresher sandwiches and other bites. Buffet tables need to be set with tablecloths and platters, and your coffee bar set with all of your after-dinner drink supplies.

Your goal, of course, is to walk into your party-ready place along with guests and have minimal setup tasks.

Clean and stock all your bathrooms with toilet paper, and set out guest hand towels the day before, wiping down sinks and cleaning mirrors so that your home is entirely prepared for a party.

A big issue with at-home parties is damages. Red wine stains on your beige carpet are going to need treatment immediately. At my own engagement party, we saved the day by having a bottle of stain remover spray handy, and it took out a huge red wine spill from our beige couch and carpet. Keep stain sprays and wipes at the ready, because tired, drunk, and careless guests may drop food, desserts, and drinks on your belongings.

Watch Out!

On a more serious note, you need to protect yourself from damages if a guest falls on your property and gets injured, or if someone drinks at your place, then drives and gets into an accident. It's strongly advised to get an additional insurance rider for your at-home event, working with your insurance provider to create a customized plan for your full protection.

If your party will be taking place outdoors, be sure your terrace, pool area, and other backyard mingling areas are clean and party-ready; that includes clearing your lawn of anything a pet dog may have left behind. Guests don't always stick to paved areas or patios, and you don't want a mess tracked into the house.

Entertainment

If your party takes place out at a bar, check ahead to see if you like the entertainment booked for that night. Most bars and lounges will post the names and websites of the musicians who will be playing that evening, and you can get a sneak peek at their acts on their sites and on YouTube. Be aware that some bars will have cover bands performing, so that might be good news if your group loves, say, Bruce Springsteen and a Bruce cover band will be performing that night. It might not be such great news for your particular crowd if the link on the bar's site delivers you to the site for a heavy metal cover band your group won't enjoy.

Money Mastery

Contact a local university's music department to inquire about hiring a talented music student to play at your party. Young musicians and singers are always on the lookout for performance events where they can gain experience and referral letters as part of their credits lists. Many ask if they can record their performance as part of their portfolio as well. Don't insult the performer, though, by not offering to pay, claiming the experience is their reward. Ask what he or she charges before the audition. It's sure to be a modest fee. Other sites to find hireable performers include coffee shops and bookstores, where many greatly talented performers work, hoping to land just your sort of opportunity.

Bars also have special events nights, such as karaoke nights, which might be fun for your group. But if the event of the evening is a beer pong competition, the place might be too packed with drunken fraternity boys for your group's comfort. Many bars also air sporting events, including playoff games that could have the bar packed to capacity with rabid, face-painted fans, and your group might not be able to get a table. Always keep an eye on what's going on entertainment-wise at the nightspots you have in mind.

For your at-home party, your entertainment might be your iPod set in its dock, with your playlist providing the soundtrack for the party, or you might set your television to a music-only station playing Top 40 songs, easy-listening music, jazz, country, or other types of music. You just leave it on in the background and you don't have to worry about entertainment the whole night.

At a booked party room, the trend is to bring in live entertainment, such as a deejay who can spin slow jazz music for your group's winding down cocktail party, or in earlier hours, perhaps that fun deejay can play club music for your VIP group to enjoy on your own private dance floor. And in a small party room, your iPod can provide fantastic free entertainment, perhaps a playlist that matches the theme of your party.

Décor

Décor for an after-party is almost always minimal, except in the case of that formal catered party hosted by a parent, the one with the ice sculptures, the light show, and the photo booth. All you'll need at an at-home party is a small low-set floral centerpiece with flowers found at the supermarket, nursery, or warehouse store for under $15, and several small bunches of flowers in bud vases set around the room.

You can create the same budget centerpieces for your booked room after-party, going to the craft store for $3 glass vases that guests can take home or that you can hold onto and use for your future parties. Leave the larger décor schemes to the bride and groom, since you never want to outshine anything they did for their other wedding weekend events.

CHAPTER 10

The Morning-After Breakfast
(and Other Breakfasts and Brunches)

In This Chapter

➤ Breakfast events for all tastes

➤ Mixing it up for breakfast and brunch

➤ Tips on planning your morning-after feast

The morning-after breakfast has for years been planned and paid for by the bride's parents, but in today's more personalized wedding world, it's entirely acceptable for the bride and groom to host their own, or for the groom's parents to host it if the bride's family wants to host the rehearsal dinner instead. Grandparents, godparents, and friends also can host the traditional morning-after breakfast or brunch, inviting guests who are staying in the hotel to enjoy a morning meal get-together.

This chapter will show you the multiple breakfast-planning opportunities you can choose from—since everyone needs to eat the most important meal of the day on each of the wedding weekend days—as well as inspiring menu ideas and planning tips.

Multiple Breakfast Events

If you'd like to host a breakfast event, but the parents of the bride or groom are already hosting the morning-after brunch, you still have opportunities to plan one of the most budget-friendly, crowd-pleasing events of the weekend.

The Morning of the Wedding

The ladies are getting ready in one location, and the men are getting ready in another location. Both groups need breakfast. As nervous as they might be, it's important for all to get something in their stomach, keep their blood sugar stable, and get the nutrients that will keep them from passing out at the altar or getting drunk from a few sips of champagne.

So it's become a trend to plan a wedding morning breakfast at the bride's location, while the groom and his men also get treated to a hearty breakfast, either at the hotel room where they are, or at a local restaurant or diner. Often, hosts order an array of food for the bride's location, then select from it to fill an oversized basket with tasty muffins, bagels, fruit salad, and other items, bringing that special delicious delivery to the groom and his men, wherever they may be.

At either location, don't try to plan a sit-down breakfast at the ladies' locale, since the morning of the wedding will be much too hectic. Hair stylists and makeup artists often arrive three to four hours prior to the ceremony to get everyone's updos in place and makeup perfected. And if the bride hires just one hairstylist to work on her, her bridesmaids, the flower girls, and the moms—as is a common budget-saving practice these days—that hairstylist is likely to arrive six hours early to create gorgeous looks for all. With hair and makeup in action, a sit-down breakfast just isn't going to be possible.

Watch Out!

Don't forget to send plates, napkins, and cups with your food delivery volunteer. Those are the most often forgotten items in the men's breakfast package.

Instead, set up a breakfast buffet on a kitchen counter or the kitchen table—or on a desk or dresser if the ladies will be getting ready in a hotel suite. Presentation is key, so line up platters and baskets to hold fresh bakery items, and pour juice into a glass pitcher for a pretty presentation. The coffee maker should be humming nearby, as well.

As the ladies move through the various stages of getting even more gorgeous, they can step to the buffet to pick on fruit pieces or pop a mini muffin. Finger foods, including bagels cut into quarters, is often the most realistic presentation for this busy scene, since it can be unlikely that anyone from the bride to the bridesmaids to the mother has the time to sit down to enjoy a full-sized bagel. And many event planners say they don't want their brides or bridesmaids cutting full-sized bagels with a sharp knife, risking cuts to their hands and resulting blood stains on their dresses. So keep everything small.

The men's buffet too can offer finger foods, although they do have more time to eat a full-sized muffin or a breakfast sandwich. But care should be taken to create an attractive presentation of their breakfast foods as well.

If you're the host of the morning-of breakfast, get the official guest headcount from the bride before ordering or making your breakfast items. Many brides' families are also present at the bride's home location, and some parents invite the grandparents and other special guests to join them for the morning-of breakfast. It may seem chaotic to have so many people underfoot when the bride is trying to get ready—and when the photographer is there posing her and her ladies for photos—but the family breakfast is a tradition in many families and in many cultures. So don't assume it's just the bride and the bridesmaids.

Get a headcount for the groom's gathering as well, since the groom might invite his out-of-town friends to his location for breakfast, which is a common trend when the men go out before breakfast to play a round of golf together. Grooms would find it rude to tell their out-of-town friends they have to leave now so that their groomsmen can eat breakfast.

Another possibility is that the bride and her bridesmaids will eat breakfast at the beauty salon where they will have their hair and makeup done. Many salons and spas offer brides the opportunity to bring in their own breakfast catering and champagne, which the salon employees will set up as a pretty buffet, including a floral centerpiece. As the ladies wait for their turn in the stylist's chair, they help themselves to the grapes, berries, mini muffins, nut bread squares, and mimosas on the buffet display. This is an efficient idea for many brides whose early ceremonies mean they have only a few hours to get ready before the wedding begins. Breakfast served at the salon is an indulgence and often a necessity when everyone must rush back to the house, dress, pose for photos, and pile into the limousines to get to the wedding on time.

Money Mastery

Pick up ready-made breakfast platters, including muffins, bagels, breads, and spreads, at your local warehouse store, such as Costco or Sam's Club, at a price that often beats bakery costs.

If you're the host of the morning-of breakfast, always get clear instructions from the bride about where it will take place, and—important!—be flexible and understanding if the frazzled bride tells you the day before the wedding that the breakfast will now be held at the salon, not at her house, because of time. That happens quite often, and the best hosts roll with the change in plans.

What about hotel wedding guests' breakfasts at the hotel? Many hotels offer free continental breakfasts in their lobbies, which guests can enjoy, or they can venture away from the hotel to enjoy a diner or restaurant breakfast with friends or relatives. It's not a must for the bride and groom, or for any other host, to pay for a morning-of breakfast for guests, but many wedding couples are quite graciously including breakfast bars and gift cards to the local Dunkin Donuts, diner or restaurant, or even including a gift card to the hotel restaurant in guests' welcome baskets.

It's also become a trend for local relatives or friends to host a breakfast on this day, inviting in-town guests to come to their homes or out to a restaurant for breakfast. Guests are likely to make enjoyable plans on their own, perhaps even gathering in one guest's suite and ordering a sumptuous breakfast via room service.

The Morning After the Wedding

The traditional morning-after breakfast takes place at the hotel, where the bride and groom, their immediate family, and the hotel guests sit down to enjoy the morning meal together. The hotel might host an elaborate Sunday brunch featuring a gourmet array of breakfast foods, omelets, a carving station, hot chafing dishes of salmon or chicken, a salad bar, and a lavish dessert spread including pies, cakes, cookies, mousses, Jell-Os™, tarts, and ice creams. On a non-holiday weekend, this type of brunch is often wonderfully affordable at $12 to $15 per person in many areas, and if you speak to the hotel's special events manager, you may be able to get your wedding group a discount on your brunch tab.

A sensational advantage to the hotel brunch is that a glass of champagne or mimosa is often included, and coffee is free. If guests wish to order an additional mimosa, that comes at an extra charge—so suggest that all guests agree to the mimosa or champagne even if they don't want it so someone else at the table can drink their share.

The hotel may give your group a private dining room, or give you several long tables in a private section of the restaurant so that your party has a defined space. And it very often already has small floral accents on the table, eliminating the need for you to spend money and time on décor, although you may wish to bring in a floral centerpiece for the main table.

The breakfast or brunch held at the hotel's restaurant, or at a nearby restaurant that guests can get to easily—meaning not a half-hour's drive away—means that many party details are covered by the establishment, not any worry of yours.

If, however, you'd prefer to host the morning-after breakfast at your home, you will need to tackle such tasks as ironing tablecloths, setting tables, creating a buffet, prepping and serving food, and decorating. Some party hosts love all of this, and choose this style of party because entertaining is a joy of theirs. Some party hosts choose this style of party because it allows them to show off their new kitchen or home décor. And some are so good at budget entertaining that even with the expenses of décor, they can beat the per-person price charged by the hotel.

If you'll be hosting this party at home, do yourself a favor and start the breakfast at 11 am or so to give you plenty of preparty hours to prepare your menu, set up, decorate, and get yourself ready. An 8 am start time is way too early, for you and for guests who may not wish to awaken at 6 am, after partying at the reception and after-party.

Your at-home breakfast menu should keep ease in mind. Avoid any menu items such as omelets or pancakes that would require you to stand at the stove preparing meals plate by plate. Quiches are a wonderful option for hot breakfast dishes, since they are easily popped into the oven six at a time, then pulled out to place on trivets for guests to serve themselves.

Additional Weekend Days

For a destination wedding's five-day length, or if bridal party members arrive two days before the wedding, plans may be set for additional breakfasts. You can host at your place, or take guests to a local restaurant. At a destination wedding, you may be able to plan a breakfast cruise on a yacht or catamaran, circling the island and taking in gorgeous scenery as you all enjoy chef-prepared hot and cold breakfast items, fresh tropical juices, and tropical fruits.

Steal My Party Idea

"We set up a cereal bar, piling up those fun little boxes of cereal flavors that our guests said they haven't had in years. We set out cereal bowls and pitchers of 1% milk and skim milk for guests to make their own cereal mixes if they'd like. That was something the kids enjoyed so much, too!"
—Renata, bridesmaid

Breakfast and Brunch Menu

Traditional Breakfast

You've enjoyed the traditional breakfast menu items for years, and the new trend is to serve classics like scrambled eggs alongside unique twists on classics such as scrambled eggs blended with red and green peppers and Monterey Jack cheese. It's not an omelet, it's a scramble. And that's how to make a breakfast or brunch buffet stand out.

Additional traditional items and their unique twist counterparts are:

➤ Bacon and turkey bacon

➤ Sausage and turkey sausage

➤ Feta and spinach sausage

➤ Pancakes and blueberry or Craisin™ pancakes

➤ French toast and crème brûlée-flavored French toast

➤ Waffles and whole grain waffles

Baked Items

Quiches are the gold standard of the breakfast and brunch worlds, with such flavors as bacon and cheddar, spinach and ham, broccoli and white cheddar, and sausage and white cheddar leading the quiche parade, to guests' delight—since quiches are not something they make for themselves very often.

Steal My Party Idea

"I had a pile of Dunkin Donuts gift cards that I got for Christmas, since everyone knows I pick up my morning coffee there, so I used those cards to get free donuts and muffins for the party, only I picked up unique flavors that people don't choose every day, such as pink frosted donuts and bear claws, low-fat blueberry muffins, donut sticks, maple-frosted donuts, and other flavors."—Melanie, bridesmaid

Relatively new to the scene is the veggie lasagna, featuring traditional lasagna strips filled with creamy cheese blends and broccoli, cauliflower, zucchini, and spinach—a crowd-pleaser for the vegetarian set.

Breakfast burritos, filled with scrambled eggs and cheddar/Monterey Jack or pepper Jack cheese with a sprinkling of sausage or bacon may be presented fresh from the baking tray onto your buffet.

And, of course, *baked* includes bakery items like bagels in every flavor from whole wheat to pumpernickel to onion to everything, muffins in every flavor from blueberry to banana nut to pumpkin (a hit at fall weddings!), breads in every flavor from banana to cranberry nut to blueberry, home-baked brownies and cookies, and everything that Entenmann's has to offer!

Don't forget the spreads for those bagels, mixing in flavored cream cheeses like chive and salmon with the standard low-fat spreadable cream cheeses. A trio of spreads pleases guests far more.

Breakfast Sandwiches

Some regions are known for their breakfast sandwiches, such as New Jersey's famous pork roll, egg and cheese sandwich on a hard roll, and you can get creative with the breakfast sandwich platter, mixing up bagels as the bread, turkey bacon as the meat, switching in spicy pepper Jack cheese, using only egg whites for the egg part, or leaving the egg part out entirely.

Another twist on the breakfast sandwich is the personal breakfast wrap. Your fix-it-yourself bar provides soft flour tortillas, scrambled eggs, veggies, cheeses, salsa, ketchup, and other toppings, and guests make their own wraps.

Cold Dishes

Create platters covered with slices of fresh fruit, including cantaloupe, honeydew, pineapple rings, strawberries, and more. When you take the time to create a unique presentation of fruits—rather than the usual cubes found in salad bars—you create a more elegant, expensive-looking display. Fill small bowls with raspberries, mandarin oranges, papaya, and other fruits that guests also don't get for themselves everyday.

A smoked salmon platter adds class to any brunch or breakfast spread, and in the refrigerator section of your supermarket, you'll find smoked salmon pinwheels filled with flavored cream cheese or goat cheese, another smart twist on the usual salmon platter. Please both traditional and adventurous guests by creating a platter of both types.

A simple bowl of cottage cheese set on ice and surrounded by fruit toppings is a hit at breakfast buffets, since some guests have cottage cheese every morning, and they won't have to commit to buying a big tub of it at the supermarket. So including that dish lets them keep their routine. You can also fill an icy bowl with an array of unique flavors of yogurts in their original little containers, also letting guests pick out their favorites, and then spooning in nuts, berries, or wheat germ for a healthy breakfast treat to balance out that bacon you have on your buffet table.

Sweets

What could be more elegant than chocolate-dipped strawberries? A platter of berries dipped in dark chocolate, milk chocolate, or white chocolate, and then dipped in mini chocolate chips or sprinkles, creates an extra-special dessert tray that's a treat or the bride and her bridesmaids. You might make your own inexpensively using a can of choco-melt that you'll find in the produce section with instructions on microwaving the chocolate and dipping berries for expert-looking results. Or you might purchase pretty bridal-themed dipped strawberries in bridal white, iced with a little pink flower, or in pastel pinks or light greens, even berries dipped and artistically decorated to look like mini brides and grooms.

If you'd like to DIY desserts for the bridal breakfast, an easy and inexpensive option is baking cookies or brownies from scratch, or using ready-to-bake packages in the refrigerator aisle of your grocery store. Give those chocolate chip cookies a bridal accent with your own packaged sugar-paste daisies from the baking aisle, or drizzle white-dipped berries with melted pastel chocolates (which you'll find in the candy-making section of the craft store.)

Kids can get into the DIY spirit a few days before the wedding, helping to pour melted chocolate into candy-making molds found at the craft store in an array of bridal or themed shapes, including hearts or butterflies (perhaps the bride's favorite!), and these home-made treats can then be used as platter décor for baked treats or toppings for iced cookies, brownies, or cakes.

Planning Tips

In addition to planning a pleasing menu for your at-home breakfast or making reservations to a wonderful hotel or restaurant brunch, other essential planning tasks need to be considered.

Invitations

Invitations to a breakfast or brunch reflect the brightness and sunshine of a new day, as shown in smiling sun faces on many cute invitation cards. Check out the breakfast and brunch invitations on Evite and Pingg, and don't forget that graphics from other categories may work beautifully for your breakfast invitation design. For instance, I've found pretty floral images and designs in the Easter section that I've used for breakfast or brunch invitations. Daisies, roses, tulips, daffodils—they all lent themselves perfectly to my spring and summer breakfast get-togethers.

An important requirement for including the location of your event—whether it's at a restaurant, at the hotel, or at your home—is including the entire address, including the zip code. This has become a new must so that guests can enter complete locational data into their GPS systems and be led directly to your party's setting. GPS systems in cars and on smartphones are wide reaching, but it's still important to enclose a directions card in your invitation for those who do not have a GPS, or whose GPS is out of order, or whose cell phone is out of juice, and so on. It's the sign of a smart and savvy party host to include printed directions. Please do keep this in mind for all types of wedding weekend events mentioned in this book, as well as for future parties and events you'll plan.

Some brides and grooms send out a reminder e-mail to their guests with a link to their personal wedding website, and to those who are invited to the morning-after or other brunches, they add a separate note with the URL of the Evite page. "Please let us know if you can join us for breakfast!" is a proper note to pair with this URL. If, as is quite common these days, you do not get an RSVP from select guests, it's okay to resend the note via Evite's resend feature, or to resend your e-mailed invitation.

Steal My Party Idea

"My group did most of their invitations via Evite, so I decided to hand write invitations to the wedding morning breakfast on pretty cards and mail them to my bridesmaids as a sweet little detail. They said it's been forever since they received a hand written invitation, and they were really impressed that as busy as I was, I took the time to write out invitations for them."—Jalison, bride

And lastly, provide dress code information, if it applies. Some hotel restaurants have a no-jeans policy, so include on the invitation the line, "The restaurant has a no-jeans policy, so here's the dress code for our party—ladies: dresses or khaki capris and sweaters; men: khakis and button-down collared shirts." Guests won't be offended by these instructions, which many guests appreciate knowing about so that they don't suffer the humiliation of being turned away at the door or feel uncomfortable in a formal setting. Country clubs and golf clubs have stated these dress code rules for years in adherence to their etiquette codes, and most guests will be aware of that, thanking you for looking out for them.

Décor

Breakfast and brunch décor is most often subtle and small, consisting of low-set floral centerpieces and floral décor touches, and the color scheme may be all white to convey a wedding tone, if that's your vision, or you may follow the larger trend and use lots of color. Most breakfast hosts ask the bride and groom to select their color palette, giving them the chance to use colors they might not have been able to incorporate into their wedding day décor. For instance, if a bride loves yellow, but her groom's family's culture says that yellow is a negative color for wedding ceremonies, she may be fine with leaving yellow out of her reception décor when she knows that her morning-after breakfast will be colored with her favorite shades of butter and bright yellows mixed with summery oranges.

If the breakfast you're hosting takes place at a restaurant or hotel, talk with the manager to find out what they can place on your guest tables as centerpieces. Some establishments will order low-set floral pieces for your tables' centers, and some will let you know which floral designers in town they commission to create their special event floral décor. They might not let you bring in your own centerpieces, so ask before you order any.

Money Mastery

Ask the hotel special events manager or restaurant manager if they have a supply of centerpiece bowls, candelabras, or platters that you can use for your party's décor. Many establishments have cases of brass candelabras or silver platters in their storage rooms or basements—many left behind from other weddings and parties—that they'll be happy to let you borrow and set out on the morning of your breakfast party. Managers know that if they make you happy by letting you borrow their supplies, you'll tell everyone you know how fabulously they treated you. That's the best form of advertising possible for them! And you can save $100 or more through your borrowed, not bought, décor items.

Toasts

As host of the breakfast, you get to make the first toast to the happy couple. No one else can make a toast until you do—according to proper etiquette—so make yours at the very start of the party. Clink your spoon on your glass to get everyone's attention, ask everyone to raise their glasses in a toast to (bride and groom's names) and offer a wonderful short and sweet toast.

Some tips for your toast:

➤ Speak slowly and calmly, even if public speaking makes you nervous. Be mindful of not rushing through your words, and you'll sound more polished.

➤ Address the day's event. For instance, if you're the host of the morning-of breakfast, wish the bride all the best for her dream wedding day, and wish her a lifetime of happiness with her groom. At the morning-after breakfast, raise your glass to the bride and groom, thanking them for honoring all of you with the chance to share in their big day, tell them it was a beautiful wedding and a sensational reception, and you wish them a lifetime of happiness, health, abundance, and laughter together.

➤ Humor is good! If you're known for your sense of humor, bring it into your toast. Not all wedding toasts have to be sentimental, teary-eyed speeches. This light and airy breakfast is the perfect time for a light and funny toast, especially on the morning of the wedding when the bride and groom are nervous and need a laugh.

➤ Toast yourselves. If you're the bride and groom hosting the morning-after wedding, it's a wonderful touch for you to stand, ask guests to join you in toasting your beautiful wife or handsome husband, and then toast the guests for coming all this way to share your day with you.

➤ Keep it short. When a toast-giver speaks for too long, more than a minute or two, it comes across as though they want attention, want to hear themselves speak, want the spotlight.

Cameras

Place single-use cameras on guest tables so that breakfast guests can snap photos from your lovely light-filled breakfast party. If it's the morning-after breakfast, it's best to put out fresh, unused cameras so that guests don't feel like you're finishing up the film in the cameras from yesterday. You can use a camera or two from the day before, though, finishing up the ones that have a half dozen shots left on them. Keep those in a separate location, like in your kitchen cabinet, or in an oversized handbag or tote.

CHAPTER 11

Casual Cookouts

In This Chapter

➤ Where to have your cookout

➤ Best foods to grill

➤ Drinks to quench your thirst

➤ Last but not least party details

One of the smartest strategies for planning a fabulous wedding weekend event is to provide a casual celebration to offset the formal wedding parties, and the casual barbecue is the top-ranking party style. Let the wedding menu have its caviar and soufflés; your crowd-pleasing party will offer pulled pork sandwiches, St. Louis ribs, turkey hot dogs with all the fixins, and watermelon or grilled pineapple rings for dessert. All of which your guests will enjoy out in marvelous weather, dressed-down and relaxed, taking a break to play badminton or dive into the pool.

This chapter takes the classic barbecue party and inspires you to dial up the creativity factor on your cookout celebration. Here, you'll find lists of the traditional dishes served at generations' worth of backyard barbecues—the ubiquitous hot dog, hamburger, and potato salad, for instance—and

Steal My Party Idea

"I knew that my son wanted to have a casual wedding, preferably a backyard cookout, but a nice one with tents and catering. The bride wanted to go more formal with a ballroom wedding, which I understand completely, so we offered to host our son's dream backyard barbecue as the rehearsal dinner—a nice, relaxed cookout with fantastic catered food. Hey, we wanted to make the groom's wedding dream come true!"—Lila, mother of the groom

you'll then find lists of the new gourmet twists that barbecue hosts now love to insert into their crowd-pleasing menus.

This section will guide you through each step of planning your barbecue party, from the all-important menu and drinks suggestions to inexpensive yet mood-setting décor, invitation trends, and play-if-you'd-like activities for the full cookout experience.

The Perfect Location

The most relaxed barbecue events take place at someone's home so that guests have access to lounge chairs and comfy seating, as well as an air-conditioned home and real restrooms, as opposed to portable or public restrooms at a park.

The Home Setting

If your home isn't a natural fit for this barbecue—perhaps your yard is small or you live in a condo or apartment with just a terrace or your spacious yard needs a lot of maintenance to level a bumpy, muddy, root-filled surface—you can check with relatives and friends to see if anyone with a lovely backyard would like to co-host this event with you.

Steal My Party Idea

"Our parents' and grandparents' generations used to host annual family picnics, and over the years as everyone moved to different states, that tradition faded away. So we decided to bring it back for our wedding weekend, and the older generations loved that we embraced their tradition once again. We're even planning to have a family barbecue next summer!"—Iliana, bride

Many people spend thousands of dollars to design their backyards as extensions of their living rooms, so to speak. Fabulous stone porches, outdoor sound systems, outdoor kitchens and bars, and the finest of patio furniture are their big home makeover project. This party counts as a wonderful occasion to show off their fine new living environment while they provide an upscale setting for the bride and groom's party. Their pool and hot tub cannot be outdone by any local resort, and their nighttime lighting system would allow for the party to extend well into the evening hours. There's no better place to host this event.

Just be sure to create a plan for a rainy day, including indoor décor and shelter for those manning the barbecue grills outside. And accept the fact that an indoor-outdoor party is likely to cause guests to track some dirt and mud indoors. A quality rug stain cleaner such as Resolve is going to be your post-party cleanup saving grace.

A Park Setting

On the flip side, you might decide to host this party at a public park, where charcoal grills are in place, benches are set on mulch-covered dining areas, gazebos offer shade, and everyone has access to softball parks, horseshoe pits, playground equipment, a swan-filled lake, and other scene-setters.

Your Best Barbecue Menu

It's time to talk about the food. A brilliant barbecue or cookout has the menu at its center, the one thing guests look forward to most, and the element that makes or breaks the party. Serve great hamburgers, and your party will be a hit; serve bland hamburgers, or burned ones, and your party flops. In this section, we go beyond grilling times to inspire you with menu items both traditional and tweaked with a gourmet twist. Highlight or circle the ideas you love, and you're already starting to create your crowd-pleasing barbecue menu.

Speaking of catering, you'll now find catering operations that specialize in barbecue menus, delivering all you need to host a traditional burgers and hot dogs cookout, a pig roast, or any other type of grilling gathering. Most packages include chafing dishes with Sternos˚, paper plates, plastic utensils, and moist towelettes for sticky-hand cleanups after the meal. Some companies will, for your guest list larger than forty or fifty people, offer you bartenders and servers, plus their grill masters whipping up perfectly basted and perfectly cooked dishes. So consider this: would you like to have a serving staff doing all the work at the party, or will you be happy prepping, cooking, serving, making drinks, cleaning, getting more ice for those who need it, making sure there are enough beers in the cooler, and so on? Sometimes it's worth it to spend extra on servers and expert help at a home-based party.

Money Mastery

Hosts who shop for party foods and party platters at discount warehouse stores like Costco and Sam's Club say they save a significant amount of money. Many admitted that they had to be convinced to try discount hamburger meat, but that they found the quality to be superior to other brands they tasted. So don't count out the warehouse store. If you or a friend has a membership, this one-stop shop can help you cater your cookout for less.

Grilled to Perfection

Your menu starts here, with the proteins. For each category, I've listed the traditional first, and then the gourmet twist that many guests say meets their dietary requirements and preferences. "I didn't expect to be able to enjoy the barbecue foods this much!" says a mother of the bride who eats gluten free. "They really paid attention to offering some healthier versions of the usual cookout fare." That's our goal—to offer both classics and twists that makes every guest happy.

➤ Hot dogs. Classic: beef hot dogs; gourmet twist: chicken or turkey hot dogs

➤ Hamburgers. Classic: beef hamburgers; gourmet twist: turkey or chicken burgers, plus gourmet burger flavor mixes like spinach and feta, or chicken, spinach, and garlic

➤ Veggie burgers: Classic: frozen garden burgers; gourmet twist: fresh veggie burgers made from julienned zucchini, onion, carrot, and other garden ingredients, portabello mushrooms as meat-replacement in a burger, or bean burgers with guacamole.

➤ Sausage. Classic: pork sausages; gourmet twist: sausages made from gourmet blends of chicken, turkey, or pork mixed with apple and maple, or feta and spinach. Gourmet meat departments also have seafood-filled sausages for a unique indulgence.

➤ Chicken. Classic: chicken legs or quarter chicken; gourmet twist: chicken legs, wings, breasts, or quarter chicken marinated in a Thai ginger sauce, teriyaki sauce, hot spicy sauce, Cajun sauce, or other sauce or rub mix

➤ Ribs. Classic: racks of barbecue sauce-painted ribs; gourmet twist: St. Louis ribs, short ribs, Asian marinated ribs

➤ Kebobs. Classic: chicken, beef, or pork kebobs skewered with onion and red pepper; gourmet twist: Yakitori chicken, beef, or pork kebobs with pearl onion and pineapple, or shrimp kebobs with pineapple, lamb kebobs with dill sauce, all-veggie kebobs

➤ Seafood. Classic: salmon steaks; gourmet twist: salmon grilled with ginger Thai sauce, teriyaki shrimp, scallops, lobster tails, crab claws

Serve an array of these proteins, with four or five different meat dishes, two veggie dishes, and a seafood dish to give all guests a fabulous selection. One of my favorite surprise barbecue entrees is a make-your-own soft taco bar with freshly grilled chicken, beef, and marinated cod. Just grill the meats in grilling baskets, and set out a five-choice toppings platter with soft tacos.

Hot Side Dishes

The menu is just beginning. The dishes around those great grilled entrées elevate your cookout to the "best barbecue ever" stratosphere. Here are the top hot side dishes to make inside and bring outside, or to heat up on your gourmet grill's side burners:

➤ Fresh buttered corn on the cob

➤ Corn and sweet onion bread pudding

➤ Baked beans, classic, or gourmet cinnamon molasses baked beans

➤ Beer battered onion rings

➤ Yukon gold french fries, classic or fancied-up with sweet potato or waffle fries

➤ Grilled squash and peppers with oregano, garlic, and lime

➤ Yukon mashed potatoes

➤ Baked jumbo russet potatoes with classic and gourmet toppings such as bacon bits, shredded Jack cheese, salsa, sour cream, yogurt, and more

➤ Mac and cheese, classic or gourmet with bacon and smoked cheddar

➤ Chili, classic or veggie chili

➤ Green bean casserole

➤ Collard greens

➤ Buttermilk cornbread with roasted jalapenos

Cold Side Dishes

Barbecues of yesteryear featured tossed green salad and potato salad, nothing more—and guests would be thrilled to find nothing less. Now, the gourmet barbecue offers a range of healthy cold salads, and some not-so-healthy creamy cold salads as well. Here are the top cold dishes to add to your barbecue menu:

➤ Tossed salad, classic

➤ Tossed salad, gourmet: chopped romaine, apple, and endive salad with white cheddar dressing

➤ Caesar salad with fresh gourmet croutons

➤ Antipasto salad with roasted red peppers, parmesan cheese, salami, and ham

➤ Three-bean salad with roasted onion vinaigrette

➤ Potato salad, classic or gourmet with peas, eggs, and crème fraiche dressing, or German-style with red potatoes

➤ Sauerkraut and potatoes

➤ Cole slaw, classic, or slaw made with shredded broccoli and carrots

➤ Cuban style slaw with jalapeno, cilantro, orange, and lime

➤ Macaroni salad, classic

➤ Seasonal fruit salad with honey, lime, and ginger dressing

➤ Marinated tomato and citrus salad with orange balsamic dressing

➤ Orzo salad with roasted vegetables and red pepper pesto

➤ Thai noodle salad with peanuts, sprouts, and red curry

➤ Pinto bean and corn salad in Italian dressing

➤ Fresh sliced watermelon

➤ Fresh pineapple cubes or circles

➤ Fresh cantaloupe cubes or half-moons

➤ Fresh fruit salad with strawberries, blueberries, and blackberries

➤ Ambrosia salad and retro Jell-O™ molds

Theme Menus

Inspired by theme menus planned for wedding cocktail parties, here are some delicious combinations that might comprise a theme barbecue:

Island Luau BBQ:

      Kahlua-drenched pork
      Guava teriyaki chicken
      Tahitian rice
      Island cane sugar pineapple baked beans
      Tropical fruit salad of mango, guava, papaya, and pineapple
      Hawaiian sweet bread and butter

Caribbean BBQ:

      Jerk chicken with mango and Creole BBQ sauce
      Calypso-grilled shrimp with citrus avocado salsa
      Crispy coconut crusted mahi mahi skewers with passion fruit aioli
      Fish tacos with island guacamole and pineapple bits

Mango red cabbage slaw
Jalapeno corn bread

Latin BBQ:

Latin chopped salad with chili lime dressing
Smoked shrimp and potato taquitos with salsa verde
Cuban pulled pork with citrus garlic
Argentinean Angus steak chimichurri
Peruvian red beans
Grilled sweet peppers with garlic and chili
Masa flat bread with herb dip

Down-Home Texas Country BBQ:

BBQ pork spare ribs
Hickory smoked chicken with coffee molasses BBQ sauce
Seasoned pinto or black beans
Classic potato salad
Grilled and buttered corn on the cob
Chopped salad with fresh veggies and white cheddar dressing
Country rolls and butter

Southern Traditional BBQ:

Kentucky style braised beef brisket with black strap molasses
Bourbon apricot glazed ham steaks
North Carolina hush puppies
Maple pecan cole slaw
Cobb salad with hickory-smoked chicken
Soft rolls with butter
Sliced watermelon

Asian BBQ:

Korean style beef ribs
Thai grilled chicken mango kebobs with red curry
Jasmine rice
Warm edamame and orange salad
Vietnamese cabbage slaw with lemongrass
Ginger biscuits
Tropical fruit salad

Appetizers

You might not think that a barbecue would feature appetizers, but even at the most laid-back cookout, the smart chef has a smattering of appetizers and platters on hand for guests to enjoy while the grilling is in process. After all, you never know when a slab of ribs will take a half hour longer than expected to fully cook, and that delay could throw off your lineup of grilled kebobs and veggies. So with a collection of tasty appetizers, guests won't go hungry.

Here are some classic and gourmet appetizers to consider for your wedding weekend barbecue:

➤ Pigs in blankets

➤ Cheese and salami pinwheels

➤ Layered Mexican cheese dip with whole wheat nacho chips

➤ Smoked cheddar cheese dip with nacho chips

➤ Classic tortilla chips, salsa, and guacamole

➤ Shrimp cocktail with mild and spicy cocktail sauce

➤ Classic vegetable crudités platter with choice of dips

➤ Buffalo chicken wings with celery, carrots, and blue cheese dip

➤ Southern hush puppies

➤ Corn and andouille sausage fritters

➤ Deviled eggs, classic or smokey-style made with andouille sausage

Watch Out!

Serve all cheese-based dishes inside the house. Baked Brie, cheese cube boards, Gouda and apricot, and creamy garlic spreads will quickly spoil when left out on a hot day, and soft cheeses have been known to make guests very ill, including posing life-threatening dangers to pregnant guests and to those with compromised immune systems. So keep those cheese dishes indoors, preferably on cooking plates or on ice for ideal cold temperatures. Even room temperatures can make soft cheeses dangerous.

The classics mix with the gourmet appetizers, and additional party appetizers may be served inside, safely out of the hot sun.

Delicious drinks

A hot day's cookout requires plenty of thirst-quenching cold drinks. The average barbecue host lines up those insulated coolers and loads them with different types of beers, sodas, and especially water. In this section, you'll get inspirations on additional drink options for your party.

Beer

Supply plenty of regular and light beers, and also add into your collection some interesting summer ales and flavored beers from top-name microbreweries. A favorite among women is the Blue Moon beer that's sweeter than the average beer and is served with a section of orange in it.

Frozen Drinks

Get out your blender because your guests may want a frozen margarita or two. Piña coladas and daiquiris are also welcome on your cookout drinks menu, providing tropical tastes and brightly colored drinks to serve in colorful glasses with fun straws found at a party supply store.

Soft Drinks

Those who do not wish to partake in alcoholic beverages and those who wish to enjoy a sweet sip between beers will enjoy your collection of unique soft drinks. Add to your cooler of sodas some fruit-flavored organic drinks such as pomegranate soda, ginger soda, black cherry cola, or other tastes from Steaz.com and FizzyLizzy.com.

Money Mastery

Ask a friend if he or she has a margarita machine on hand that you can borrow for the party. (Of course, this friend has to be invited to the party!) You can rent these machines from party rental agencies, or you can decide to buy your own if you foresee many other summer cookouts in your future, but the smart decision for your budget now is just to borrow the machine.

Another favorite at barbecues is the pitcher of sweet tea paired with a pitcher of unsweetened iced tea and a pitcher of flavored iced tea such as peach or berry. You might blend up several bright fruit juices and pile in slices of fruit for a nonalcoholic sangria. Lemonade is a favorite at cookouts, too, in classic lemon or pink lemonade form.

Frosty Drinks

If the temperature isn't scorching hot, you can serve ice cream sodas, ice cream floats, root beer floats, and even ice pops as thirst quenchers. These frozen drinks can pair with fruit salads or colorful fruit kebobs as the healthier alternatives in your dessert lineup that can also include cupcakes and cookies, ambrosia, ice cream sandwiches, or shaved flavored ice in colorful cups. You can borrow an Italian ice maker too.

Additional Party Details

With your party's menu in hand, look now at the additional essential details of the party. Here is where you'll explore some creative options for planning your party's fun atmosphere, sharing your party's theme and details with guests, and planning activities for all to enjoy.

Décor

Balloons have long been the traditional party décor for this type of party, with bright oranges, reds, and yellows reflecting the summery theme. And since it's not a rule that this party can take place only in the summertime, consider a fall color scheme of deeper reds, oranges, and golds that reflect the leaves in the trees, bringing Mother Nature's décor scheme into your party and letting her foot the bill for the décor all around you.

Watch Out!

If it's a windy day, those balloons are going to be a menace. If the wind is blowing, just bring those balloon bunches indoors to decorate the inside tables where guests may be likely to gather in the air conditioned interior of your home.

Keep your décor budget to the elements of your buffet table, with a colorful tablecloth and coordinating plates, bowls, and cups, all from a party supply store bought with a coupon, of course, for 20 percent or more off the list price. You'll find tiki bar-themed tableware as well as solid-colored plates and napkins to place on a themed, patterned tablecloth. Having patterns on both tablecloth and the plate on top of it creates design overkill. It's always better from a decorator standpoint to choose just one patterned décor piece for your buffet.

Cover each of your guest tables—borrowed or rented—with tablecloths of the same design. A bunch of colorful balloons held down by weighted bases provide the perfect festive décor for your party.

Invitations

Don't just send invitations with a barbecue graphic on them, since guests may take that as just a summery theme and not an indication that the party's outside and they should dress for the weather. Instead, use that summery graphic, or a solid-colored invitation in bright orange or yellow or pink, and include the words "Please join us for a barbecue at Stacy and Bill's house! Dress for sunny weather, and leave those stilettos at home."

The other portion of barbecue invitation musts is letting guests know if they need to bring a bathing suit and towel for your swim party. Just add a line at the bottom of the invitation reading, "Sundresses and shorts are the dress code, but bring your bathing suit and a towel for a dip in the pool!" Most guests may know that Stacy and Bill have an amazing backyard pool with slides and a waterfall, and that swimming is always an activity at their parties, but you may have some guests on your list who are new to your group, perhaps in-laws of the bride and groom or long-distance friends who know nothing about Stacy and Bill's lavish outdoor oasis. Guests will appreciate that you're keeping them in the know so that they won't feel disappointed and left out when they arrive.

The top summer graphics used on barbecue invitations include beach balls, palm trees, tiki heads, coconuts, beach umbrellas, colorful flip flops, and a full smiling sun. For that autumn barbecue, the top graphics are footballs and football goal posts, and autumn leaves.

Activities

If there's a pool on the premises, you might keep your party to a unregimented, no-activities mood, letting guests just float in the water, swim on their own, or relax in the hot tub. Or, you might organize an in-water volleyball game, swim races for the kids, or float races for both kids and adults—or kids versus adults.

Outside of the water, consider planning these top yard games, all easily propped with inexpensive game kits found at Target, Toys"R"Us, Kmart, and other inexpensive stores:

➤ Volleyball

➤ Wiffle ball

➤ Kickball

➤ Bocce

➤ Horseshoes

➤ Water balloon toss

Water-based games are especially enjoyed by guests on a hot day, so stock up on super soakers and watch those eyes light up when you bring out your arsenal of neon-colored

Watch Out!

Speaking of land mines, if you have a dog living on the premises, be sure to make a careful sweep over the entire lawn – back, side and front – to remove any dog droppings. And if you don't have a dog but your property is often visited by deer, make sure you do the same. Guests running around barefoot would not enjoy stepping into a surprise, and you also don't want the disaster of a guest tracking a mess inside your house.

water guns for all. Water gun fights get everyone running around, so of course it's best to allow this activity if your yard is flat and clear, not a minefield of tree roots, holes, and other ankle-twisting dangers.

Be sure to plan indoor activities in case a rain storm, oppressive heat, or cold weather forces your party indoors. Collect an array of fun games, such as Scene-It™ or Pictionary™ for guests to discover on a table and begin their own group play. Movies or sporting events can play on your big-screen television, and don't forget that guests don't need to play at your party. Most will be overjoyed to just have mingling time with other guests, enjoying your spectacular menu and drinks.

And, of course, the big draw for kids: the rented inflated bouncy house. Contact a reputable rental agency—every parent you know will be able to suggest the one they've used for their kids' parties—and choose from a castle, a tropical island setting, a dragon, a pirate ship, or other fun designs. With parental supervision, the little ones will jump inside those inflatable fun houses for hours. And if the bride and groom wish to climb inside, that makes for great photos from your sensational party.

CHAPTER 12

Sporting Events

In This Chapter

➤ His side vs. her side sporting events

➤ Sporting events for a team of one

➤ Planning tips for your sporting event

With so many of the wedding events focusing on food and drinks—cocktail party canapés, pigs in a blanket, cheese platters, martinis and Mojitos—everyone's going to want to get some exercise to burn off those fat grams and rejuvenate their energy levels. So that's makes this chapter's event style one of the fastest-rising trends in wedding weekend activities. More and more hosts are planning sporting events for everyone to participate in—or cheer for from the sidelines.

Here you have the opportunity to plan either a team sporting event like a softball or basketball game with the groom's side taking on the bride's side, or an individual sporting event like golf or tennis—and even those two can be turned into a his-and-hers tournament.

Before you start thinking about sporting events that you'd like to plan, keep one important timing factor in mind: always plan a sporting event for the day after the wedding. This is not one to plan for the day prior, since you don't want the bride or groom (or anyone else) taking an elbow to the face, getting scraped up, turning an ankle or getting any other type of sports injury. "We thought a day-prior basketball game would be fun," says Emily, a bride. "But my groom went up to take a shot, knocked heads with the guy who was blocking him, and we wound up in the emergency room for his concussion. A pretty bad one, too. The doctor told him not to fly, so there went our honeymoon." *Ouch!* Keep all sporting events to the day after the wedding, and brides and grooms need to play conservatively and protect themselves.

Read on to explore the different types of sporting events that you might plan, and choose one that most guests can participate in. You may be planning for a wide range of ages and exertion and skill levels, and don't forget that kids will want to play as well.

His Side vs Her Side Sporting Events

The bride and groom have just combined their families by getting married, but you can still plan a his side vs her side sporting competition, with the groom's friends and relatives forming one team, and the bride's friends and relatives forming the other team. If one side is short players, volunteers can play for 'the other side.'

Some party hosts go all out, getting personalized team T-shirts made up. The bride's side and groom's side each choose a team name, and we've seen everything from Annie's Team and Doug's Team to creative team names like The Crunch Bunch and The Diamond Dolls. "We came up with three possible team names and e-mailed them as part of our invitation, asking guests to vote for their favorite team name," says Cathy, a bridesmaid. "That got everyone excited to play."

Steal My Party Idea

"We had a lot of kids on the guest list, so we alternated every inning of our softball game. The adults played an inning, then got some rest and drinking time while the little ones went onto the field to play some T-ball."
—Sally, bride

What to Play

Here are the most popular sporting events chosen for his side vs her side competitions:

➤ Softball

➤ T-ball—everyone plays, and it's harder than it looks!

➤ Mini golf

➤ Flag football or touch football

➤ Ultimate Frisbee

➤ Basketball

➤ Bowling

➤ Wiffle ball

Wiffle ball is supremely popular for group sporting events, since the plastic bats and balls can be purchased at Target, Walmart, Kmart, Walgreens, Toys"R"Us, and other stores for just a few dollars. And you can play in someone's large backyard, rather than try to find a park nearby. (And getting a permit to use it! We'll talk about locations in a bit.) Wiffle ball enthusiasts may already exist within your group, and they may have all the gear you need. And a game of Wiffle ball is so much fun to watch, since a great pitcher of that hole-punched ball can put dramatic curves on every throw. Everyone gets to show off their batting and fielding skills as well, and little ones can easily play. Plus, if you're in the backyard, you're very close to the refreshments up on the deck or inside the house—not to mention the restrooms.

Also popular for backyard team sporting events are the perennial picnic and family reunion favorites:

➤ Bocce ball

➤ Horseshoes

➤ Beanbag toss

➤ Egg toss

➤ Water balloon toss

These no-impact/no-sweat games may be ideal for the older generation to enjoy and show off their impressive skills—especially in a bocce game where grandpa and the great-uncles get to revisit the favorite game of their youth and impress everyone with their finesse and back-spinning tosses. Grandparents say they love getting to play a sporting event with the kids, and these activities are fun for all ages.

Turning It into a Tournament

As host, you have your option of game length and style. You can plan a single softball game, with winner taking all, or you can make it a three-inning round robin tournament in which each game ends after three innings, and the winners of each game play each other. The losing teams play each other in a battle for the bottom—letting four or more teams battle it out for the first annual title. That's right—these games and tournaments very often turn into traditions in the family and among friends. At the next wedding to take place,

Shop Here!

Order your kids' and adults' team logo T-shirts from CafePress.com. Unlike many other personalized shirt companies out there, these shirts are well-constructed cotton and sizes are true to national size standards. You can design your team shirt and set up a free e-store for everyone to buy their own, and you can get hats and water bottles featuring the same logo you design.

Watch Out!

If you have anyone in the group who's known to be—how shall I say this—aggressive in their playing style, taking it way too seriously, getting angry, insulting people, it may be better to plan a noncontact sporting event. Talk to the bride and groom if you're not familiar with their entire circle of friends and family to ask if this might be a better idea for everyone's safety and the fun of the group.

the bride and groom might do the same thing, spurring a rematch among their circle of friends.

No matter what the sport—rom basketball to boccie—you can create a tournament and encourage good-natured trash talking between teams and players.

Individual Sporting Events

Another possibility is skipping the big group sporting competition, skipping the his side vs. her side organization, and just planning an outing where guests play a particular game. You might just announce that your event is a trip to the local high school tennis courts, where everyone can just spend the morning playing singles or doubles they match up themselves. Golf or mini golf are also tops in the individual sporting event category, and twists on other sports such as a game or tournament of H-O-R-S-E (a basketball-skills shooting game, with everyone shooting baskets from different positions) or a football-throwing skills competition lets everyone play for fun (and perhaps prizes).

Event-Planning Tips

Now that you've been inspired by different types of sporting events that may be your chosen event to host, you'll find the following top planning tips helpful.

Location

Choose a location that has all you need. A public park has one or more basketball courts and tennis courts, but be aware that these can be taken by other park goers. So don't choose a

Steal My Party Idea

"A friend of ours is a member of a country club, and he helped us offer a morning round of golf for anyone who wanted to play. He arranged for guest passes once the RSVPs and payments came in, and they all went off to play golf at a gorgeous course that many of the guests said they always wanted to play. It was a highlight of the guests' weekend, and the groom loved playing with the bride, the dads, his boss, and his friends as well."—Atienne, bridesmaid

busy park or playground, or plan to send out a "court-sitter" an hour or so before the party to reserve the space, playing there until your group gets there.

Some public spaces will require permits for use, and this category often involves tennis courts, school fields and tennis courts, and park game fields. You don't want your party shut down by the park service or police because you didn't get a permit. Check with the township about the need and process for getting permits, which often cost $20 or so. Towns especially require permits and your ID in case the field gets damaged or if anyone gets injured while playing on town property.

A home setting is often easiest and most comfortable, since you'd have access not just to an available area to play—such as your yard or driveway basketball hoop—but to a restroom and to indoor air conditioned areas on a hot day, both very important considerations. Another plus is that you'll be able to grill on your own grill and prepare and serve food and drinks much easier at a home setting than you would carting everything to a park or field.

Invitations

Send these out early, months before the wedding so guests can arrange their travel and lodging plans to still be in town on the day after the wedding when the big tournament will take place. Guests will also need to know about the sporting event in question so they can pack the appropriate sporting outfit, sneakers or spikes, and gear like a baseball glove, batting or golf glove, and other essentials. Guests who don't have advance notice of this type of wedding weekend event would be so disappointed if they couldn't participate for lack of needed gear or outfitting!

Have some fun designing your invitations. Evites and other online invitation companies have ready-made designs, such as invitations featuring bowling pins and balls for your bowling party, or basketball and football designs meant for playoff and Superbowl parties, and you can use those theme invitations for your event. Again, Evite.com's online announcement and visual RSVP list keeps you organized and lets all of the guests see who's attending (or not).

If you'd rather send print invitations, you may be surprised to find that your word processor's clip art has the perfect sporting icons for your homemade invitation design. Center the image

Money Mastery

Check the website for the sporting establishment, such as a mini golf place or a bowling alley. Many now have free invitations that you can print out and send.

of those bowling pins at the top of the invitation page, and there's your only needed graphic for the invite. Your printed information follows.

Your word processing program likely gives you the opportunity to print out your design on regulation postcard size, which you can create on ready-to-print postcard card stock from an office supply store. When you're creating postcards, always print on heavy card stock, since the post office won't mail regular paper cut to postcard size.

For the wording portion of your invitation, have some fun with it and generate enthusiasm. Here's an example:

It's On!
Join us for a his side vs. her side softball game
on Sunday, June 16th at 1 pm
at Lincoln Park—group rides departing from the hotel
RSVP to Cindy at 973-555-0202 by June 3rd

Or

Will you Wiffle with us?
Jake's parents are hosting a Wiffle Ball tournament
at their home on Sunday, June 16th at 1 pm
We've got the bats, you bring the battle!
RSVP to Jim and Marcia at 973-555-7653 by June 3rd

A line on the invitation works best to let guests know what they need to bring. Here's an example:

We have the bats, balls, and bases,
And team T-shirts are here for you to change into.
The rest of your gear is up to you!
Bring a water bottle! It gets hot here in the afternoon!

Gear and Supplies

Recruit friends to help supply you with the equipment you'll need, such as several basketballs, a bocce ball set, horseshoes, footballs, and more. Usually, a network of friends will have the gear that's needed, so you don't have to spend a fortune at the sporting goods store.

One cute idea is to take a separate basketball or football—not the game ball that will get dirty and sweaty—and have all of the guests sign it for the bride and groom using a Sharpie with black or colored ink. The ball becomes a keepsake for the happy couple.

In addition to the equipment you'll need for your game, be sure to pack the following essentials for everyone to share:

➤ A first aid kit

➤ A cooler with lots of bottled water and energy drinks on ice

➤ Sunscreen

➤ A sporting single-use camera to capture fun images of the game without risking damage to expensive digital cameras.

➤ Game day snacks, such as sunflower seeds in the shells, a favorite at baseball games, or Cracker Jack. Another game day favorite is orange slices kept in a sealable baggie in the cooler.

Food and Drink

Your location is going to determine your food and drink plan. If you're playing in a backyard, then it's quite easy to plan a barbecue and set out a buffet on the patio table with drinks served at your outdoor bar or from coolers. If you're in a public park, you'll have to adhere to the park's rules, which may be that food and drink is allowed only in the picnic area or that food and drink isn't allowed without a permit. You can't just fire up your portable grill in the parking lot, or the police will ticket you.

If you're at an establishment like a roller or ice rink or bowling alley, of course you have access to their restaurant for pizzas, chips, nachos, pitchers of soda, beer, and other food and drink. And some establishments will allow you to bring in your own food items. Just call first about the food rules so you're not turned away by management when you walk in with $100 of food and drink only to find out that outside food isn't allowed.

The most common menu style for sporting events is tailgate party fare—hot dogs, hamburgers,

Money Mastery

In the case of ice skates, bowling shoes, and other rented gear, just let guests know on their invitations that "Shoes cost $2 a pair to rent" and they'll know the cost is up to them.

Money Mastery

Compare prices to see which of your local supermarkets has the best prices on hamburger meat, buns, and the rest of your catering order. Supermarkets now have their own apps that you can check to compare prices from your smartphone, and coupons are always brilliant for saving on big food orders. Visit Coupons.com and the other coupon sites listed in the resources to snag big savings on your grocery shopping trip.

chicken, potato and macaroni salad, green salad, watermelon—and, of course, you can get more creative with gourmet burgers and veggie burgers to please your foodie and vegetarian friends.

Of course, drinks will be on the menu, and twelve-packs of sodas and water bottles are the best way to go even if they cost a little bit more than big jugs of water and big bottles of soda or iced tea. Provide enough soft drinks for everyone to drink at least four apiece, especially on a hot day. You don't need to pull out the hard liquor for this event; a variety of beers— both regular and light—arranged on ice in a drink tub or cooler is the most popular crowd-pleasing drink plan. And you can save on your drink purchases at a discount liquor store, where prices may be 10 percent less than at your usual supermarket.

Finally, desserts are always welcome at sporting parties, but for ease of serving, offer handheld treats such as cookies, brownie squares, and cupcakes, all of which can be smartly decorated in the sport's theme—such as cupcakes iced to look like baseballs, or brownies cut into the shapes of footballs. These little theme details impress guests and show off your hosting skills.

If you'll be serving cake or desserts that require a plate and fork, visit a party supply store to get a few packs of cute themed plates such as ones with a football or basketball theme. You'll even find plates with a horseshoe on them, meant as a good luck symbol but perfect for your horseshoe party in the backyard.

If you have several co-hosts, ask each of them to bring a platter of desserts as their contribution to the party. Most co-hosts would far rather make something than hand over their share of the cost, since they know how to bake on a budget.

Steal My Party Idea

"Since the wedding was in the fall during playoff season, we were so happy to see that our supermarket had football-shaped cakes in its bakery section for a really low price. So we just grabbed one of those, and we were all set!"—Dania and Tom, bride and groom

Ask a clerk at your grocery store bakery section to see when they'll have sports-themed cakes, or if they can make you one.

Prizes and Trophies

Make it extra fun by giving out prizes to the winners of your sporting competitions. You can get fun little plastic trophies at party supply and craft stores for about $1 each. For free, you can print up award certificates, making one set with his side named as the winner, and one set with her side named as the winner. Then just grab the right packet to hand out to the team.

Add another layer of fun by presenting prizes in different categories. For instance, your mini golf tournament presents the opportunity to hand out prizes for Hole in One, Best Comeback, Best Trick Shot, Best Abuse of the Obstacle (for the person who kept hitting the windmill!), Best Back 9, Best Sportsmanship (for the person who cheered for everyone), and Worst Sportsmanship (for the person who jokingly trash-talked the competition or cheated on a shot). Gather everyone together to hand out the prizes, which can be as simple as certificates and as theme-matched as a pack of three colored golf balls or—my favorite—a yo-yo for the person with the lowest score (as in find another hobby). If you have kids playing, it wouldn't be nice to give this last prize to one of them, though. Instead, have a special prize for the winner among the kids, and individual prizes for all the kids for doing so well.

Cheering Section

Add some extra excitement to your sporting event by having some guests act like cheerleaders. Your cheering section can wear matching custom T-shirts as they clap, spell, and perform the cheers they remember from their school days. Youngsters can put their hair in ponytails and be the cheerleaders for their sports-playing parents, waving the colorful pom-poms you buy at toy stores or sporting goods stores (or make as an easy DIY project). At one weekend sporting event, the grandmother generation volunteered to be the cheerleaders as their husbands played bocce, and the entire group loved it.

Lastly, take plenty of pictures during your sporting activity to be shared with all in attendance at this fantastic wedding weekend sporting get-together, as well as with those who wish they had joined in the fun.

Adventure Outings

Guests who love an active lifestyle and adrenaline-soaked activities will love your ingenuity in hosting an adventurous outing during the wedding weekend. What's most fascinating about this style of event is that party hosts draw inspiration from the wedding's location. Some brides and grooms live in a certain city because of its wealth of hiking, biking, climbing, and boating opportunities, and when you tap into their hometown's adventure opportunities, you honor them as a couple as well. For destination weddings, the couple has chosen their locale for its beauty and for its exotic adventures such as snorkeling and volcano hiking, activities they'll love to share with their wedding guests during an outing planned for after the actual wedding day, when a skinned knee won't be a wedding day disaster.

This chapter lists some of the top adventure outings and adrenaline sports planned by today's wedding weekend event hosts, and it will also help you put this outing together with a collection of smart tips, musts, and warnings.

Watch Out!

As you review this list, keep in mind the availability of the gear needed for the outing. Can guests bring their mountain bikes or climbing gloves? What's the cost of using a resort's kayaks or boats? Many party hosts are beating the high costs of getting gear by renting their equipment at their local REI store, which rents kayaks, canoes, and other sporting goods. Find your local store through REI.com.

Types of Adventures

Some adventures you can embark upon on your own, and some will require the assistance of a professional guide found through a tour company that conducts hikes, climbs or rides led by experts. These companies welcome your group with an essential training class, where the pro will assess your group members' skill levels and special needs, choose a path that suits your abilities, answer your questions, and outfit you with the correct protection gear. These guides accompany you on your trek, adjusting your path and making your outing even more fun with anecdotes and FYIs about the flora, fauna, and sea life you encounter along the way.

Again, always choose an activity that your group is skilled and healthy enough to undertake and enjoy.

On Land

These land-based events range from simple hikes through wooded paths or along coastlines to dream-come-true adventures such as riding horses on a beach. Here are ideas suitable for every season:

> ➤ Rock climbing
> ➤ Biking
> ➤ Horseback riding, trail
> ➤ Horseback riding, on a beach
> ➤ Hot air ballooning
> ➤ Snowmobiling
> ➤ Cross-country skiing
> ➤ Downhill skiing
> ➤ Snowboarding
> ➤ Hiking a challenging hill or path
> ➤ Hiking, cave exploration
> ➤ Hiking, tours of ruins
> ➤ Hiking, waterfall tour
> ➤ Rainforest canopy, or zipline, tour

On the Water

The following adventures may put your group on the clear blue waters of a tropical ocean or gliding through a wildlife-filled river path or past billion-dollar oceanfront mansions, historic lighthouses, or seals sunning themselves on rocks. Or, you might find yourselves in the water, swimming with sea turtles and snorkeling through iridescent schools of fish. Here are the top choices in water-based adventure outings:

➤ River rafting

➤ River tubing

➤ Kayaking

➤ Canoeing

➤ Riding a Jet Ski

➤ Speedboating

➤ Parasailing

➤ Snorkeling

➤ Swimming with dolphins

Scuba diving is only a realistic idea if everyone in your group is already trained and certified to dive those shipwrecks off the coast. Scuba classes take time, and your group might not wish to learn anything new, or take on the challenge of scuba skills at this outing. An easier form of underwater exploration, such as snorkeling, may be your best bet.

Planning Tips

Since adventure sports and outings do carry an element of risk, with guests out in nature on paths they're not accustomed to, it's smartest to take a few extra planning steps to ensure everyone's safety as well as their enjoyment. Here are some essential planning tips to keep in mind.

Get a Guide

Check the websites of adventure sports companies carefully, and always choose the company that offers a reputable guide. Your local REI store can connect you with the most respected, best-equipped adventure sports companies in your area, and some REI stores employ the very same guides who work at those tour companies, are accredited, and know your region best. It's never a good idea to head out on a dangerous tour with an inexperienced sporting enthusiast who isn't the best person to protect your group, or without any guide at all.

Timing Issues

For any adventure outing, the weather will be a factor. Hiking won't be fun, and will indeed be dangerous, during a heavy rainfall or days after a snowstorm when the path has been packed down into a sheet of ice by other hikers. Humid summer days in the tropics could make outdoor exertion potentially more dangerous, with even your fittest group member getting dehydrated and close to heatstroke. So always let the weather help you choose your activity.

Some seasons are better than others for wildlife spotting, with certain birds or sealife more plentiful during certain months. And, of course, the fall months have you biking or hiking through trails with trees that are in full autumn colors of bright oranges, reds, and yellows. Destination weddings may be located in a region where you don't know what the weather is like, so you might not be aware that July is peak season for enormous mosquitoes or sand flies. Checking with the tourism offices of any location is the best way to investigate the season, and all of its challenges, for outdoor activities.

Watch Out!

It's not enough to have a map or a printout of tour paths that you've printed out from the Internet, since paths may be changed or may have experienced erosion that makes them dangerous...a fact that a website hasn't included. An actual expert is a very smart addition to your group.

As mentioned earlier in this chapter, you don't want to plan this outing for the day before the wedding. A scrape, bump, or bruise will spell disaster for the bride or groom, and a turned ankle on a rocky path means one or both will be headed up the aisle on crutches. So, again, always set adventure outings for the day after the wedding.

Also honoring the wedding events, schedule this outing for a day when you have plenty of available time, allowing for an hour or two overtime in case your tour takes longer than the guidebook suggests. That is most often the case, and it would be disaster if your group was missing in action for the start of an event planned by the bride and groom. Allow plenty of cushion time, including the time needed for travel back to the hotel from the mountain, and shower and dressing time.

Legalities

Never head out into the landscape without first checking to see if you need a permit for conducting an adventure activity on park grounds. State parks have strict rules about visitor permissions, and you'll certainly want to hear from a park ranger if bobcats and mountain lions have been spotted in the area. Always conduct a thorough search through the park agency commission to find out the current permit requirements, application process, and fees.

As you investigate permits and other legalities, you'll also discover one piece of information that has tripped up hosts who have planned evening adventure events: the park might close at sundown, and your group might find a locked gate blocking your exit. Plus tickets on each of your cars. Don't forget to check the hours of any park or sporting company to avoid headaches and extra expenses from having to return rental equipment the next day for twice the price.

What to Bring

It would be unwise to lead a group out into nature without bringing along the top essentials. Here you'll find a smart packing list for the supplies you'll need, and that your guests will thank you for, during your adventure outing:

➤ Water: Bring lots of water to stay hydrated and energetic, and also to clean off any scrapes you may get while biking or hiking. As you're exerting yourself and sweating, your body needs to replenish fluids, so make sure your group has enough bottles of fresh drinking water for each person to drink several bottles' worth during your outing.

➤ Food: Pack baggies of energy-boosting trail mix, nuts, or other protein-rich snacks, rather than sugar-laden bars, cookies, and junk food. Even for a brief two-hour boat ride, exertion is likely to be higher than you expect, so it's always smart to have an easy edible on hand.

➤ First Aid kit: Make sure it's new, not the one you've had in your car for five years, so that medications within it haven't expired. And if the park ranger office sells snakebite kits, buy one and bring it along. Better safe than sorry.

➤ Animal protection supplies: If your locale is home to a population of large predators such as bears or even mountain lions, it's smart to bring along the protection gear that your park ranger recommends. For

Watch Out!

If all of these warnings about large predators—plus poisonous snakes that live in desert, mountainous, and even residential areas—make you nervous about dangers to your group and to yourself, it might be best to take your adventurous spirit indoors, perhaps to a rock climbing gym, where you can all harness up and race to the top, safe from bobcats and rattlesnakes.

some animals, an air horn is enough to scare them off. For others that don't react to noises, such as snakes, you'll need a lesson in what to do and not do should you cross paths with a dangerous animal. And, again, a snakebite kit is a wise addition to your backpack if you're going hiking or climbing in a region that's home to snakes.

➤ Cameras: You're going to be in gorgeous scenery, and you may see amazing things such as rainbows over waterfalls, a doe and her fawn just a short distance from your hiking path, breathtaking views of the ocean vista. You're also sharing this experience with friends you haven't seen in a long time, perhaps on your first adventure together in years, so you'll want plenty of photos and video of your outing. So bring along a top-quality single-use sporting camera, such as the new Kodak models, to snap fantastic photos of your trek without putting your pricy digital camera in danger from dirt or water. And bring along a camcorder to capture those once-in-a-lifetime moments such as seeing dolphins swimming alongside your boat, or capturing a friend's dive from your boat into the crystal clear ocean.

➤ Cell Phones: WiFi is everywhere, so bring your fully charged cell phones so you can call for help, if needed, or be reached in case of an emergency back home. Your phone may also have a GPS app that could help your group find its way back to the rental company. "We spent all day out on the lake, and we would have had the worst time finding our way back to the boat rental place at the end of the day when we were all tired and sore. The GPS on my friend's phone saved the day!" says bridesmaid Cammi.

➤ Sun Protection: I saved the most important for last. Bring along plenty of different kinds of high-SPF sunscreen, such as sprays or creams, and use them liberally on your body, face, lips, and even the top of your head. And it's a smart idea to tell your guests to bring along their own hats to protect them from the hotter-than-expected sun and guard them from skin damage.

Invitations

Your invitations can be easy Evites, or you can design theme-matched invitations, such as one featuring a photo of dolphins, with your message of "Come swim with us! Sarah and Devin invite you to the adventure

Etiquette Friendly

As a reminder, it's essential to let guests know what they'll need to pay for, if anything. So include a note that clearly spells out the fact that they'll have to pay for their own rentals. "We've arranged for discount group rates, so your boat will only cost you $15 to rent for the day! Please send Katie your payment via check or PayPal by April 12th, and call her at 675-555-8754 if you have any questions."

of a lifetime: a swimming with dolphins outing at DolphinQuest on the day after the wedding!"

The top invitation designs for this type of wedding weekend outing feature graphics of scenery that's similar to what guests will view while on the outing, images of the sporting equipment such as a top-tier mountain bike or Jet Ski, and photos of the bride and groom enjoying an adventure of their own. The latter pays tribute to the couple's love of sporty outings, and personalizes your invitation with their image, giving guests the message that they'll share this activity with the bride and groom.

Guests will need as much information as possible, so provide the link or URL of the tour guide company, and spell out the details of what guests need to know. You might write, "Bring your biking gloves and gear, we're renting bikes there!" or "Sneakers only on the boat; the captain forbids any wedges or heels on the schooner, for everyone's safety!"

 **Playing Tourist**

In This Chapter

➤ Touring a city's history

➤ Finding movie and TV filming locations

➤ Restaurant dining

➤ Planning tips for tourists

When you plan an afternoon of visiting tourist spots in an area, you add an exciting, unforgettable element of local flavor to the wedding weekend—setting a sense of place and sharing all of the most amazing sights and tastes of your region. What's most amazing in this trendy event style is that both long-distance and local guests get just as much enjoyment out of this tourist hot spot activity. "I've lived an hour outside of New York City all my life, and I've never been to the Statue of Liberty. So it was just as much fun for me as it was for my guests from Kansas, Chicago, and LA," says Dena, a recent bride. You'll find that's the case a lot of the time: locals just don't do the tourist thing unless they're taking out-of-towners to see landmarks.

In this chapter, you'll explore some of the biggest draws for a playing tourist wedding weekend activity, and you'll learn smart tips for making the tour even more memorable.

Historic Landmarks

No matter which city you're in, there are impressive landmarks to show your guests. In Chicago, it may be Harpo Studios. In Boston, it may be Fenway Park. In New York City, it may be Rockefeller Center. A Washington, D.C., wedding will bring you to some of the most amazing buildings and statues ever created. All of your guests will enjoy a late-morning to afternoon tour of these sites, whether on a touristy double-decker bus or with a walking tour led by you and your handy guidebook or an app designed to guide you around the city and share factoids about the landmark you're at.

In a smaller city or town, you'll also find fascinating landmarks and tourist attractions. Just contact the local tourism board and historical society to get not just a list of landmarks, but their history and even maps for self-guided walking tours.

Steal My Party Idea

"I visited the historical society's website and saw that they had walking tours of historic haunted homes, which was perfect for our October wedding."—Laura, bride

Historical societies often offer guided tours with themes such as revolutionary war landmarks, haunted tours, and tours of celebrity homes.

In tourist areas of even small towns, you'll find a list of historic tours. During a recent visit to Cape May, New Jersey, I found a guided tour operation that offered trolley tours of historic pirate spots along the coast, as well as haunted Victorian home tours and military history tours. Trolleys make for great group tour vehicles since not everyone wants to walk for miles on a hot day, and some guests may have mobility issues. Look for trolley tours that can keep your group together. As romantic and fun as a horse and carriage ride is, it splits your larger group into groups of four or so, and it can be a lot pricier than the trolley tickets.

View or Enter

When it comes to skyscrapers, lighthouses, and grand mansions, you have a choice to make according to your group's wishes: do you view the landmark from the outside, or do you pay the ticket to go inside? It's a smart idea to give your group the option. Some can climb the two hundred plus steps to the top of the lighthouse, while the rest explore the gorgeous gardens below and tour the lighthouse museum on the first floor. Everyone gets the experience they desire.

Take a Guided Tour

Before you buy tickets for a guided tour, always check to see how long the tour will be. Some tours are quick in-and-out tours of less than a half hour, which may be most pleasing to guests who don't have the patience for a long, drawn-out history lesson. And some last two hours. So get that vital information before plunking down cash and locking everyone into an educational experience that takes up a big chunk of the day.

Movie and TV Locations

"When we took our guests into New York City, they wanted to see all the places they loved from *Sex and the City*. I wish I knew that beforehand, since there are tour companies that do special tours of TV and movie-taping sites," says Brandy, a recent bride.

Some online research will also uncover the locations where movies and TV shows were filmed. One of the most in-demand locations in Hoboken, New Jersey, for instance, is the *Cake Boss* bakery, which is located just a few blocks away from the train station. People come in from states away to stand in line, take photos in front of the bakery, buy a treat, and maybe see the Cake Boss at work or taping his popular show. Many wedding groups now include a tour stop in Hoboken to give their guests the thrill of seeing the *Cake Boss* place.

Some locations provide iconic television and movie experiences, like the windows outside *The Today Show* or *Good Morning America*, where your group could see a star or two, or catch one of the free outdoor musical performances. "The kids in our group got to see the Jonas Brothers through the window," says Alison, a bride. "And I got to see Matt Lauer. So everyone was happy that day!"

Watch Out!

Don't get suckered by a flyer or ad pronouncing that a company will take you on a tour of all the sites where TV shows and movies were taped. Always research to find a reputable company recommended by the city's tourism department, at TOWD. com. It recommends the real deal.

Eateries

It might not be architecture and TV series settings that thrill your group. If you live in a culinary mecca, then your tourist itinerary may include eating at notable restaurants, such as those owned by celebrity chefs, or James Beard award-winners, or just iconic restaurants. For instance, if your group is in New Orleans, you might restaurant-hop between the eateries run by Emeril Lagasse and Paul Prudhomme. In Las Vegas, you have a wealth of celebrity chefs' restaurants to choose from. All foodies have a wish list of restaurants they'd love to visit, and your tourist tour can make their dreams come true.

And, of course, there are restaurants that represent the good life, such as 21 in New York City, where celebrities dine often. *Us Weekly* magazine is always printing the names of restaurants where the rich and famous have been spotted sharing a plate of calamari and snuggling in the corner. Celebrity spotting is a popular element of the tourist outing, after all, even when it's food on the menu. In chapter 15, you'll explore the ins and outs of the culinary tour, including restaurants owned and frequented by celebrities.

Planning Tips

Here are some musts when it comes to planning your tourist outing:

➤ Contact the tourism office of the location to ask about special discount packets given to family special events groups. Some tourism offices have actual goodie bags filled with coupons and freebies like hats and T-shirts that they give to wedding and family reunion groups.

➤ Talk to the hotel concierge to see which kinds of coupons, twofers (two tickets for the price of one to attractions), maps, and travel guides he or she can give you.

➤ Talk to the hotel manager (or have the bride and groom call) to see if your group can use the hotel's free shuttle bus for your tourist stops. Some hotels have multiple shuttle busses that they let wedding groups use, and this could be your free party bus (minus the alcohol).

➤ Check each destination for entry fees, accessibility, and other requirements for your group.

➤ Bring plenty of cameras along, including camcorders, so that you can capture iconic tourist moments like guests running up the *Rocky* stairs in Philadelphia. They'll want to post that on their Facebook pages.

➤ Let guests give their input, but to a limit. E-mail your guests ahead of time to have them vote on your list of five or six tourist spots. Always limit the selections, or else you'll be running all over the city to get to the places each person wants to see. They vote on the six, and you'll get to as many as possible before everyone gets exhausted.

➤ Don't be surprised or offended if some guests choose not to join your tour on that day, especially if the weather is uncomfortably hot or if it's raining.

➤ Bring someone who knows the city well so you don't end up hopelessly lost and frustrated in yet another subway station, with grumbling guests asking if they can just go back to the hotel.

Shop Here!

At Coupons.com, you'll find coupons for local eateries and attractions. You just enter your zip code, or the zip code of the wedding weekend's location, and click on the coupons that look applicable. Print them out, as many as you need up to the print limit for each, and don't be shy about handing out coupons to guests for their $5 off lunch.

CHAPTER 15

Culinary Tours

In This Chapter

➤ Famous and prestigious restaurants

➤ Celebrity cooking lessons

➤ How to plan for your culinary tour

Food-based wedding weekend events are always a hit with guests, since so many consider themselves foodies (aka gourmet enthusiasts in the know about different cuisines and the top-name chefs who make them). Add in the treat of getting to experience the wedding city's local flavors. As a global society, many guests live in regions where they cannot easily find, say, a great pizza or fresh seafood. A culinary tour invites guests to experience the scrumptious tastes they grew up with—and share them with their spouse or partner and kids—or experiment with an exotic cuisine.

This chapter will provide you with culinary trends in wedding weekend events, inspiring you to look at adventurous cuisines, down-home favorites, or guest-thrilling celebrity restaurant experiences. Fans of *Top Chef* may love a great foodie festival such as the *Food & Wine* Classic in Aspen (more on that in the next chapter!), but they may also know that the wedding's location means they'll be in the same town as celebrity chefs' restaurants that they've always wanted to visit. This chapter helps you locate them.

Weddings are not just family reunions; they're also a sweeping destination wedding for many guests who do not live in the same hometown as the wedding couple. When guests travel to and lodge in a couple's hometown, they look forward to trying the local cuisine, seeing the sights, making this trip a vacation of sorts, with culinary stops on their wish list. Rather than make their own way to a well-known eatery on their way home, they're excited to share the experience with other friends and relatives, thanks to you.

Notable Eateries

Foodies know their dream restaurants in any city. They follow the prestigious James Beard Awards given to top restaurateurs and up-and-coming chefs, and they dream of someday dining in a James Beard winners' eatery. A wedding weekend provides the perfect opportunity to host a handful of VIP guests at an elite restaurant that has won the "Oscars of the culinary world." Obviously, a meal at many of these eateries can easily cost several hundred dollars for a group of four to enjoy, so this outing is best kept to an extremely small group of guests.

Money Mastery

A fine dining experience at a stratospheric restaurant is a fine idea for hosting parents, to thank them for helping to plan—or fully funding—the wedding. Brides and grooms are surprising their parents with a dressy dinner at their dream restaurant, planning the event for the evening before guests arrive for the wedding weekend, or saving this exceptional dining reservation for the night after the wedding, when they have wedding money to spend, and when other guests have departed.

Famous-Name Restaurants

The wedding's location will obviously determine which famous-name restaurants you can easily travel to. If, for instance, you're in or near New York City, Las Vegas, Los Angeles, or New Orleans, you have a wide variety of famous restaurants to consider. But here's an eye-opening resource that will show you famous-name restaurants in many additional cities: Seeing-Stars.com. This fabulous website links to you to celebrity-owned restaurants all over the country. It also points you to restaurants the stars frequent, and since celebrities love the good life, their choices of eateries often list the names of the most famous-name restaurants in the world.

I also love to read the restaurant lists on TravelandLeisure.com, where you'll find its World's Best Awards listing the top-name eateries currently named as *the* place to be. *Food & Wine* magazine is a bible for locating and learning all about the top famous-name restaurants that foodies and non-foodies alike will be thrilled to experience.

Don't forget that you don't have to have dinner at these famous-name restaurants. You may be able to create a culinary desserts-only tour at these eateries. And don't forget as well that famous-name restaurants aren't always super-luxury eateries. A famous name might be the Hard Rock Cafe or Geno's Steak cheesesteaks in Philadelphia. Even fast-food restaurants count! "We took our guests to In-N-Out Burger, believe it or not, since so many of them lived in cities where that chain isn't located. But many of our friends have always talked about going to one, so we hosted them for dinner there instead of at a $200 per person restaurant! It was a huge hit!" says Christine, a recent bride.

When you are looking at fancy restaurants and award-winning famous restaurants, bear in mind that reservations can be very hard to get, requiring months of advance notice in some situations. So start your research as soon as possible to book this grand culinary adventure tour.

The Bride and Groom's Favorite Restaurants

Customize your culinary tour to include stops at the bride and groom's favorite restaurants. You can consult with the bride and groom to get their wish list of top local eateries for your culinary tour, or surprise them by taking them and their guests to the restaurants and dessert spots where they had their first date, where the groom proposed, and other locations that play a part in their love story.

Since weddings are now so creatively personalized to tell the story of the bride and groom's romance, planning a culinary tour that takes them down memory lane—and shares these eateries with their friends and family—can make your wedding weekend event extra special for them all.

Theme Eateries

Another trend in culinary tours is planning a theme outing. If the wedding's location offers a signature cuisine, such as Italian or Cajun, your tour can be planned to include several different stops at ethnic eateries in a location such as Little Italy or the French Quarter. Again, these stops don't have to be full meals, and indeed shouldn't be for guests' comfort and for your budget.

Steal My Party Idea

"We knew we could never afford to treat guests to a full dinner at the hottest restaurant in town, so we called to see about early bird dining and tasting menus that would fit our budget. We then were able to plan early-evening stops at three different famous restaurants: one for an appetizer tasting menu, one for its early bird dinner, and another for its desserts only."—Anya, bridesmaid

Steal My Party Idea

"At every stop along the way, we told the maitre d' that we were a wedding group and that the bride and groom have long been fans of the restaurant, so would the chef be available to make a quick visit to our table? 'It would make the bride and groom's day,' we said. And every single chef was willing to greet the bride and groom at our table, accept our compliments, and one even pose for a photo with us."—Celia, bridesmaid

They're just offering a taste of each spot's signature dish, and often a table visit from the chef upon your request.

If you're at a destination on a Caribbean island, you have the pleasure of giving guests the opportunity to sample island cuisine. The resort's concierge will have restaurant menus for you to browse, or you can pre-research the top eateries at the destination wedding location by reading the travel sections of bridal magazines along with your favorite travel magazines' articles and reviews. Again, don't miss out on the wealth of the World's Best Awards lists at TravelandLeisure.com, since they give awards for the best restaurants in the Caribbean or wherever you may be in the world.

Theme foodie tours may also focus on a certain type of food, such as bringing guests from hot spot to hot spot to sample the region's beignets or kebobs, turning your culinary tour into a tasting tour combined with city souvenir shopping and landmark visiting. Some of the top food-centric culinary tour themes include:

➤ Pizza, with each guest getting one slice at each stop

➤ Sliders, with guests splitting orders of four or five of these mini burgers to get a taste at each stop without getting too full

➤ Sushi, with guests sharing their eight-piece orders of hand rolls to get a taste of adventurous flavors without committing to a big order. Guests say they love getting the chance to experiment with a "scary-sounding" hand roll flavor, and health-conscious guests enjoy these brown-rice bites that are so much better for them than sliders or pizza.

➤ Kebobs, which also allow guests to sample bites of flavors they might not otherwise order as a whole meal for themselves while out to a dinner. Many guests say they discover new favorites during this type of fun foodie tour.

➤ Cajun food, a New Orleans favorite foodie tour, with stops to sample different types of beignets or small portions of jambalaya, po'boys (often available as sliders), and more

➤ Gelato, again as a reminder that it's not always bar food or dinner food at the center of a foodie tour. Hopping from gelato place to gelato place in a touristy town lets everyone sample a range of flavors, sharing a few cups with one another. Again, new favorite flavors are often discovered by all.

Foodie Events

The *Food & Wine* Classic in Aspen might be the best-known food and wine festival, thanks to several seasons of the show *Top Chef*, but it's not the only one. If you can get tickets to that celebrity-studded festival, that's quite a coup! The bride, groom, and their guests will consider it a highlight of their foodie lives, akin to attending the Oscars! But you'll likely have more success in scoring affordable tickets to the many other food-centric festivals and special events in your area. Here's how to find them:

> ➤ Check the events calendar on your regional magazine's website. Food festivals are listed there, with some of them being charity events, so check that section of the calendar as well. Top-name chefs and restaurants are often invited to showcase at culinary festivals that don't carry a $100 ticket to attend.

> ➤ Check with your local hotels. These sites are often home to special foodie events planned by townships as a way to promote local restaurants to the community. Often called Taste of (Town's Name)and often including silent auctions and buffet servings of the restaurant's signature appetizers and bites, these events are the highlight of many townships' year, and make for the perfect event to share with wedding guests.

> ➤ Check with your local clubs. The Elks Club and the Junior League often host foodie events to raise funds for different charities or simply as community events. You might attend the club's summertime pig roast and carnival, for instance, where local eateries provide their dishes gratis to the organization, and very affordably to you.

Cooking Lessons

Celebrities are hosting private parties in their homes, where personal chefs conduct fun, interactive cooking classes for their guests. Everyone dresses casually, the wine flows, music plays, and the party's in the kitchen where platters of pickings are set around the room as snacks to be enjoyed while the dishes are being prepared. Ivanka Trump recently said she hosted a Thai cooking class for her friends, and many party hosts are following her lead in planning chef-led cooking events.

Shop Here!

Check the website PersonalChefs.com to find chefs and caterers who conduct in-home cooking parties.

You can host this type of party in your own kitchen, giving your home a party atmosphere with a wonderful sense of communing in the kitchen as a talented chef displays his or her skills, and guests choose to participate, or not. It's just as much fun for guests to look on at the impressive cooking lesson taking place.

Planning Tips

The first consideration is always going to be timing. When is there a lengthy amount of time for guests to trek to the city or into town where the restaurants are? This type of outing is usually reserved for the day after the wedding, for both timing reasons and so that the wedding menu isn't outshone by a meal or treat enjoyed at a top-name restaurant by star-struck guests.

Another time when the culinary tour can work is the night before the wedding. While the bride and groom are conducting the rehearsal and hosting only bridal party members at the rehearsal dinner, you can save the day by providing a wonderful dining opportunity for all of the out-of-town guests. This only works if you're not in the bridal party yourself, so keep that in mind.

Money Mastery

Use the free map-creation website WeddingMapper. com, where you can create an account even if you're not a bride or groom. This site allows you to enter the name of each restaurant or foodie location, it automatically creates an icon on a map of the region, and you enter a note for each location, perhaps sharing the fun FYI that this is where the bride and groom had their first date. You can then e-mail the map to guests, and print out copies to use as your invitation treasure map.

Invitations

E-mail guests with your invitation to your culinary tour, and include links to each restaurant planned as a stop along your route. Guests can check out the site ahead of time, review the menu, learn about the chef and his or her illustrious career, learn about the restaurant's own rich history, and—quite importantly—get a gander at the food prices.

It's also become a trend for creative hosts to make print invitations designed to look like menus or in the form of a map studded with gold stars marking each stop along the way (or a spoon icon or any other indicator design you choose).

Evite is also a smart, free invitation tool for this type of party, allowing guests to see the lineup of stops on your itinerary, and also to see who is attending your outing. You'll find stylish foodie invitation designs here and at Pingg.com as well.

And, finally, if you'll DIY your invitations, consider printing them out as postcards in standard postcard size to keep costs down. There's no need to spend money on save the sates mailings for this event, but sending your invitation months before the wedding weekend allows guests to create their travel plans so that they can be present on the day after the wedding, or take an earlier flight to arrive in time for the event the night before. The earlier you invite guests, the better. You can then make the calls months ahead to the restaurants to reserve your tables.

Favors

No favors are needed for this type of outing, since the treat is the experience itself. But if you do wish to give guests a little something—and many hosts who plan at-home cooking class parties do decide this—treat guests to a small container of gourmet edibles that match the theme of the outing. For instance, if your culinary tour is taking you to a variety of Italian eateries, your take-home favor might be baggies of biscotti. If your tour will take you to Chinatown and its wonderful eateries, your favors can be creatively decorated chopsticks or a box of fortune cookies or Chinese spice packs. A regional food tour invites you to give local flavor favors, such as Cajun spices or maple nut bars or classic containers of Old Bay seasoning.

Since this is a foodie experience, gourmet favors are most appreciated by guests, so stick with the basic categories of food-based favors:

➤ Baked treats

➤ Spices

➤ Recipe cards

Sauces may sound like a winning favor idea, but with airline restrictions on liquids causing everyone to dump their contact lens solution at the security checkpoints, it would be a shame if guests could not bring their gourmet sauce back home with them. And packing a sauce in a suitcase is also not a great idea, since plane pressurization can sometimes cause containers to burst while in flight. No one wants to get home to a suitcase filled with clothes ruined by a pomegranate or barbecue sauce. So choose something other than a liquid favor of any kind.

And, of course, the best favor is a memory captured in the form of photos taken of guests at the amazing famous eateries you visit. Foodies love to share their big-name adventures on their Facebook pages, making them the envy of their friends. So take plenty of photos along the way, getting fun shots as well as group poses to really capture the flavor of the savoring you all enjoyed so much.

 **Festivals**

A fabulous festival or street fair has so much going on, attractions for every age. And if you're a host on a budget, this one is often free. Everyone just heads to the center of town or to a college campus or fairgrounds and joins the throngs of people gathered to enjoy the free concerts and performances, browse the offerings at the vendors' carts, and fill up on street fair foods. *That's* where party guests really have fun, since the festival's theme often calls for specialty foods such as sausage, peppers and onions, and zeppole at an Italian festival, or crawfish at a seafood festival.

This chapter describes several of the top types of festivals for your party plans, as well as how to help your group have a wonderful afternoon enjoying the attractions. But first, you have to find the festivals. Here are the top resources to check now, not just for the dates and locations of upcoming festivals in your area, but in some cases for discounted tickets and free passes to them:

➤ Festivals.com lists every type of festival you can imagine headed to your town or to a location near you that you had no idea hosted these kinds of events.

➤ TOWD.com will guide you to the local tourism boards of your town or a nearby city, or of your destination wedding location so you can check for scheduled festivals, and this is where you're going to get those freebie and discount tickets. If you don't see free tickets listed on the tourism board's website, call the board to ask for some. They often give out ticket packs to local hotels and bed-and-breakfasts, and your one call can net you a pile of free tickets too!

➤ Regional magazines and their websites list community calendars and upcoming events in their social sections, and this is where you'll find out about festivals on the way. As another perk, you can send the link to this festival right to your party guests so they will know about the celebrity musical acts and other attractions they can look forward to.

➤ Arts centers are usually involved in hosting festivals, so call your local arts center or cultural club to ask about upcoming festivals. Many celebrations are annual events, and if they're not yet up on the website, a quick call to the arts center will usually connect you with a planner who's in the know and can tell you when that festival is planned.

Steal My Party Idea

"We knew that the bride is crazy about Native American culture, so when we found out that there was going to be a big Native American powwow taking place just forty-five minutes from here, we made plans for group tickets and told everyone that it was going to be a big surprise for the bride. No one told her, and when we all drove up to the fairgrounds and she saw where we were headed, she was so happy! It was her first time ever at one of these festivals, and she had always wanted to go to one! We had the best day!"—Chrissy, bridesmaid

Seasonal Festivals

Tourism in any area depends on bringing lots of people ready to spend money into the region. And a seasonal festival can do just that. Each of the four seasons brings with it an array of activities—think ice sculpture competitions in winter—as well as seasonal foods, flowers, and symbolic performances like dance troupes doing traditional numbers for prosperity or a good harvest. Whether in hot or cold weather, seasonal festivals are so much fun for guests who might not live in a region that gets a variety of weather, thereby making the activities exciting and great photo opportunities, and for guests who just might not have ever thought to attend one.

Spring Festivals

Spring festivals are a tradition dating back eons into ancient times when the return of the sunshine after a long, dark winter called for bright and cheery festivals filled with flowers and grains symbolizing a good harvest to come. Now, those good-luck grains may take the form of warm breads sold by vendors—such is the evolution of tradition.

Spring festivals are often centered around flowers, such as Tulip Festivals and Lilac Festivals, with the celebration strewn with all manner of fragrant flowers and blooming garlands, musical performances, artists painting little ones' cheeks with tiny flowers and setting floral wreaths on their heads. Cupcake vendors set out platters of delicious treats topped with sugar-piped flowers and edible blooms, and gardening clubs offer little potted plants for purchase. Thus there's something for everyone, which makes a festival a great, affordable event for the wedding weekend.

Summer Festivals

Townships everywhere love to host summer festivals, and you'll especially see these in shore and lake towns, and on boardwalks that have lots of games and rides for all ages. The smart marketing gurus in tourism agencies love to promote summer festivals with themes such as 1950s sock hop weekends with classic cars on display, people dressed up in poodle skirts, and some sporting the greaser look. Your group can join in the costume fun if you let them know to bring their leather jackets, saddle shoes, and neck scarves. Doo-wop groups perform in gazebos and ice cream sodas are offered everywhere.

Fall Festivals

Autumn festivals, with their trees all ablaze in rich oranges, reds, and yellows, are the most popular seasonal festival. Guests love the autumn foods at these festivals, which often include clam bakes and football tailgate party fare. Some festivals are even NFL-themed for local fans to show their loyalty, and pro players show up to sign autographs and judge football-throwing competitions for the little ones and for adults. Game jerseys are worn by guests (who have been told to bring theirs!), and face-painting artists can decorate cheeks with the team colors.

Hot cider and hot chocolate are offered by vendors, as is microbrew beer in specially designated beer garden areas, and, of course, fall includes Oktoberfests with their sauerbraten and potatoes and beer, and polka bands and servers and dancers dressed in costume. Again, this festival is beloved by guests who might not otherwise plan to attend an event of this style, and it provides fabulous photo opportunities.

Steal My Party Idea

"Our nearby beach town hosts an annual volleyball tournament as part of its summertime kickoff festival, and it attracts big-name pro-volleyball players. So we planned our wedding weekend outing for that beach at that time, and everyone loved getting to see the televised volleyball tournament, getting the pros' autographs, and just playing on the beach for the day."—Elaine, bridesmaid

Winter Festivals

Ski resort towns are especially likely to host winter festivals, and with a snowy coating on the ground and trees glazed with ice crystals, the winter wonderland setting offers such group-favorite activities as sleigh rides, tobogganing, evening ski runs, snowman-making competitions, ice skating, and more. Craft vendors display at these fairs, providing plenty of fun shopping for colorful gloves and scarves, and hot drinks are available to keep frosty guests warm.

Cultural and Arts Festivals

The arts are alive and well at festivals all across the country, and your group could venture to a jazz festival featuring some of the biggest names in jazz music, all performing for free to admiring crowds. Shakespeare festivals are a favorite in college towns and other art-centric areas, with stock companies performing the Bard's classics as well as modern twists on the classics. Dance festivals have become a big trend now, thanks to the revival brought about by *Dancing With the Stars*, and one of the most popular such festivals centers on flamenco dancing with its colorful dresses and passionate performances.

Speaking of cultural centers, those are the places to contact about festivals celebrating the beauty and tastes of heritages, such as a Polish festival or a Ukrainian festival. If the heritage is the background of the bride and groom, that's a wonderful addition to their wedding weekend, an event the older generations will especially love. The younger generations will be exposed to the true nature of their background, learn phrases in the family language, taste foods they might never have had, and hear stories about family ancestors and their weddings. Some wedding weekend groups drive an hour to get to their heritage cultural festival, and it then becomes a tradition for local family to go to this festival every year from then on.

Shop Here!

Contact local dance academies and cultural centers to ask about upcoming dance festivals. They'll know when and where these events will occur, since their troupes may be invited to perform.

If the cultural festival scheduled for that weekend is not of the bride or groom's heritage, that's perfectly fine. Groups still find it tremendous fun to explore a different culture's music, food, costumes, history, dance, and legends. When you offer an event that's truly unique, guests love the novelty of it, the adventure and fun of sharing this with their kids and their friends.

"When the bride and I graduated from college, we trekked across Europe for the summer," says Elizabeth, a bridesmaid. "We had so much fun in Portugal and wished we could stay longer. So when I found out about a Portuguese festival that would be taking place during the weekend of the wedding, I knew I had to 'take her back' to our favorite country, share our stories with our friends, and taste that amazing food. She said it was the perfect ending to her wedding weekend, sharing that with her new husband and also with me and our friends."

You can find cultural festivals through the heritage association you have in mind. Just Google Italian American Association or other keyword-laden phrases to find an official group in your area. I've found great success in contacting local universities' cultural studies departments to find out about planned festivals. Colleges' heritage clubs are in the know about such events, and they'll point you to the event you're looking for. Festivals.com is also be a prime resource for finding these celebrations.

Steal My Party Idea

"We missed the Ukrainian festival in town by a few weeks, but that didn't stop us. We created our own Ukrainian festival at my house, with homemade pierogies and other authentic foods that the other bridesmaids and I cooked with the help of the moms and aunts (and the bride's dad, who makes amazing stuffed cabbage). We contacted the Ukrainian school that the bride went to and asked if we could hire some of its dancers to stop by and perform, and we were able to get them to come over. We played music, the bride danced with them—it was fantastic! And it turns out that the bride had wanted to have Ukrainian foods at the reception, but their caterer didn't offer those dishes, so this gave her what she really wanted for her wedding celebration." —Tania, bridesmaid

Plan your own cultural foodie festival by asking relatives to share their recipes or make a platter or two, and upload some cultural music to your iPod to play at the party.

Food and Wine Festivals

Guests love going to food and wine festivals, since so many people consider themselves foodies and wine connoisseurs, thanks to shows like *Top Chef*. The prize there, after all, is a showing at the *Food & Wine* Classic in Aspen, Colorado, a top-tier festival attended by the

Shop Here!

Find out about wine festivals, as well as food festivals, at WineSpectator.com and FoodandWine.com, as just two of the top great food and wine resources. And, of course, Festivals.com includes foodie and wine fests in its listings.

who's who of the culinary and wine world. Imagine the RSVPs pouring in with glowing yes! responses when you send out invitations that you're hosting a trip to *that* festival—or one quite like it.

The foodie festival is a new hot trend in wedding weekend activities, since there are so many different regional and culinary specialties celebrated all over the country. It might be a New Orleans crawfish festival or a Maine lobster festival, a French fare fest, a Tuscan-inspired food festival in wine country. Speaking of wineries, they exist all over the country, not just in Napa, and they often host wine festivals to celebrate and promote their newest vintages.

Guests who join you at these food and wine festivals can look forward to trying little plates of gourmet fare prepared by up-and-coming chefs, celebrity chefs with cookbooks to promote, local restaurant chefs, bakeries, and more. A day of grazing on wonderful bites provides a luscious, satisfying day of indulgence, and guests get to discuss their own foodie knowledge and favorite chefs, restaurants, and regional cuisines. It's like the best wedding cocktail party ever, with the illuminating experience of milling around within the cultured class of refined tastes.

"I'm a total cheese lover," says Stacy, a bride. "I'm always taking my friends to fondue places and cheese counters at gourmet markets. I had no idea there was even such a thing as a cheese festival, but my bridesmaids found one at an artisan cheese maker's family farm, and it was amazing! They had long, rustic tables set up in their orchards, and their servers walked around with platters of amazing cheeses, wine was flowing, music was playing. It was a dreamy afternoon!"

Festival Outing Ideas

The first thing you might wonder about when considering a festival as a wedding weekend event is does everyone try to stay together as a group, or can people go off on their own. It's a legitimate question, especially considering how many different types of attractions and food carts there are at a festival.

If you have a group of a dozen people or so, it's easier to stick together. Guests won't feel comfortable saying, "Hey, thanks for bringing us here! See you later!" before they splinter off from the group to go to the beer garden. Smaller groups magnetize, with everyone wanting to stick together. Larger groups of twenty or more often see groups of like-minded or like-aged people heading off on their own, perhaps to the kiddie rides (while the rest of the group goes to the beer garden.) So here's your solution: as the party host, assess the group you have with you. Is everyone similar, as in are they all college friends, or do you have several generations of people with you? Your group might be a natural fit, all wanting to hit the same attractions. Your group might be comprised of couples with little kids, singles, and people of the older generation.

One idea that works well at festivals, and is often most realistic, is to give your group a plan. Say, "Okay, we're going to start off all together for some food, and then after lunch, everyone can go to the attractions they like—the rides are over there, the beer garden over there, the shopping over there. And then at 2 pm, we can all meet up again right here for desserts. Sound good?" Everyone will love that plan, since it gives them the freedom to do the things they like, enjoy their visit, make their kids happy, do their own thing—it's much better than feeling like you're following a tour guide around. And party hosts who try to herd everyone together, forcing togetherness, come off sounding controlling and harsh—and no one has the best time ever. So let the people in your group split apart if they'd like to. Natural groupings of friends will enjoy the freedom to do so, and then everyone still gets the together time. Done.

Enjoying the Spotlight

Performances take place everywhere at festivals, and it's a wonderful idea for guests—or the guests of honor—to join in when a performer invites everyone to come up on stage for a dance or to help with a magic trick. Encourage guests to do so if they wish, but never push, and never put someone on the spot by whistling for the performer to grab the bride and groom (who would be mortified since they're not the spotlight types).

On the other hand, the bride and groom might want the spotlight, and may wear attention-getting T-shirts or hats announcing them as bride and groom. Everywhere your group goes, the bride and groom will be recognized and applauded, and don't be surprised if vendors hand them a complimentary snack or keepsake. Those perks come readily to those wearing bride and groom gear.

Shop Here!

One of my favorite sites for high-quality, well-designed bride and groom T-shirts, hats, and other personalized items is CafePress.com. Before the wedding weekend, either ask the bride and groom to pick out their favorite styles and get it for their wedding weekend event, or surprise them with a matching set of baseball hats emblazoned with script Bride and Groom on them. Café Press provides plenty of creative, family-friendly designs. Always choose a G-rated T-shirt to be worn to a public outing such as a festival.

Guests who love the spotlight can dance with the performers, sing a karaoke number, sit up front for the comedian to joke with, or participate in a competition. Take your cameras along because you're going to get a lot of fun footage and amazing photos of your group having a fabulous time at the festival.

Other ideas for your festival visit:

➤ Check the festival website ahead of time to learn the day's schedule of events, when performers will be on-stage, and other timed occasions.

➤ If you have guests in your group who have limited mobility, check the festival website or call the organization number of the festival to ensure appropriate access and ease of walking through the grounds. A wheelchair-bound guest would be very limited at a festival that is set on a bumpy, muddy fairground.

➤ Bring plenty of water bottles with you if you're headed to a festival on a hot day. You don't want guests to get dehydrated and headachy under the hot sun.

➤ Bring sunscreen with you.

➤ Bring a few little bottles of hand sanitizer for everyone to use before eating.

➤ Make sure everyone has your cell phone number and that you have theirs in case of an emergency while everyone is split up at the festival. A quick call and you can all gather to depart.

➤ If you're faced with adventurous, exotic foods at a festival, order one plate for everyone to try, and then you can order more if your group loves it.

Etiquette Friendly

As the event host, you can pick up the cost of everyone's entry tickets, if there is a fee, and then allow everyone to pay for their own food, drinks, and shopping picks. You're not beholden to pay for absolutely everything on this day. You can offer to pay for the group lunch, if you wish, but be aware that festival food prices can be surprisingly high. If you offer to pay for lunch before you get there, you might lock yourself into a very big expense. It's good etiquette to let guests know ahead of time that their entry tickets will be complimentary at this event, as a thank-you for attending, and they'll know to bring some cash along for their additional expenses.

CHAPTER 17

Seasonal Events

In the prior chapter, you looked at the different kinds of festivals that take place during the four seasons, and now you're looking a little further into the activities and opportunities that abound during spring, summer, fall, and winter to give your group an experience they'll really love, especially if they don't experience a particular season, such as a snowy winter, where they live.

In this chapter, you'll find lists of the many types of activities you might choose during the wedding weekend, and you're encouraged to revisit the early chapters in this book to figure out the basic details of your plan, such as matching an event to a time of day, choosing an event that your guests can attend and will enjoy best, and sending theme-matching invitations.

Speaking of invitations, be sure your style of self-made invitations or the designs you see on Evite.com and other online invitation sites are smartly matched to the style of the event you plan. For instance, if your event is a trip to an aquarium, find an invitation style featuring a dolphin or a whale. As a little secret to theme-matching invitation designs, be sure to check out lots of different categories of invitations, not just the ones that represent your event theme. For this aquarium trip, for instance, you'll find lots of sweet smiling dolphins and whales in the kids' party invitation section. I've also found pretty fall-themed invitations in the Thanksgiving section, even though my party wasn't a Thanksgiving event. I've also found starbursts for a summer party in the retirement party section.

Read on to discover the most popular, and most enjoyable, seasonal activities planned for wedding weekends.

Spring

Spring awakening brings with it brighter colors, fragrant flowers, lighter wardrobes, and even the return of baseball. That gets people outside, happy to be free of wintry weather, refreshed, and ready to enjoy all that springtime has to offer.

Baseball Games

Spring training has begun, and late spring presents opening day celebrations at ballparks both professional and minor-league. These early-season games are such an exciting draw for groups, and minor-league baseball game tickets are especially affordable, with group discounts offered for ten or more people in your circle. Minor-league ball games are family friendly, as well, with games and activities between each inning, rousing music playing in the stadium, kids jumping up to do well-known dances such as the "Cha Cha Slide" and the "Chicken Dance," among other numbers.

Guests with kids love having the chance to experience that ball game bliss with the little ones, munching on hot dogs, nachos, and cotton candy, running over to meet the fuzzy mascot, and even meeting players on the field to get autographs. "We don't live near a pro ballpark, and I always wanted to take my kids to a ball game," says Frank, a best man and father of three. "So when we found out the parents had planned this day-after outing, we were all really excited. It's the kind of golden memory you know your kids are going to keep forever."

Garden Tours

The rebirth and renewal of spring means cherry blossom trees are in bloom, tulip borders are bright with color, and so many breathtaking gardens welcome visitors to tour their grounds. Check with your local tourism department to discover public and state-funded gardens that you might not even know are nearby—hosts discover the loveliest places

Watch Out!

A seasonal rainstorm, heat wave, snowfall, or other extreme weather could potentially cause a disruption in your event plans. Summer activities would not be held if there's a hurricane brewing, and an ice storm is surely going to lead to the cancellation of the outdoor tree-lighting event. So always have a fun plan B in mind. Instead of going to the beach, for instance, take your group to an aquarium or—if travel is a danger or impossible—plan a movie night with summer-themed films on your playlist.

when they're researching for these events—and also ask about planned events in which private gardeners open their properties (many of them mansions or bed-and-breakfast establishments) for a day welcoming visitors to marvel over their gorgeous gardens, koi ponds, waterfalls, arbors, and more.

House Tours

Many townships, junior leagues, and other groups now offer inspiring, lovely house tours, which may be part of a fundraising event, with a nominal fee collected at the start of the walking tour. Your group gets to visit and tour the homes of the upscale elite in your area, including their gardens. Those who love home décor and home makeover shows on HGTV love getting to tour amazing homes as part of a wedding weekend outing.

If this type of event is scheduled for your particular weekend, send out an Evite with a link to the home tour site so guests can get a sneak peek at the historical homes and marvelous mansions in question. As an alternative, many tourism departments can point you toward a single impressive historic home that's available for a house tour. For instance, in Morristown, New Jersey, wedding groups love to visit the home that was a headquarters for George Washington, as well as other historic homes in the area rich with Revolutionary War history. In the south, historic home tours share that region's Civil War lifestyle and history, with tour guides showing displays of the gorgeous dresses the women of that era used to wear. In coastal regions such as Newport, Rhode Island, the mansions of the long-ago wealthy class are often open for guided tours, where your group can even learn about the grand weddings held in these breathtaking homes.

Keep in mind that all of the ideas mentioned here in the spring section are available for the summer and fall seasons too!

Shop Here!

Call your local arboretum to see if it has tours of its expertly landscaped grounds, and find out what its garden themes are. Some welcome you to tour their Asian gardens with cherry trees in bloom and bamboo forests studded with educational plaques, or their Tuscan gardens, cactus and succulent desert gardens, herb gardens, and more. Some botanical gardens in big cities are popular tourist attractions, and that might be your choice as well, but your botanical garden is also a great resource, generously sharing the locations and websites of other local floral paradises.

Summer

A summer wedding, or a destination wedding in a locale where the weather is summerlike, presents fun in the sun opportunities for your group:

Beach

There are two kinds of beach outings planned for wedding weekend events: the first is filled with activities and the second has nothing planned—people just relax on the beach and do whatever they want. If the wedding weekend is a hectic one with lots of activities planned already, the second type may be most appreciated by guests who, although they're having a fantastic time, may feel a bit run ragged by so many social events.

So, with guests advised in the invitations about an impending beach day and encouraged to bring along their beach chairs, blankets, umbrellas, and bathing suits, your choice as host is between these two styles. If you do wish to plan activities for your day at the beach, here are some ideas:

➤ Volleyball game

➤ Sand castle competition, with a prize for the group-selected winner

➤ Beach football or soccer

➤ Kite flying, especially during a late afternoon to evening trip to the beach

If you're at a destination wedding or are lucky enough to have access to a beach with phenomenal waters and reefs, your group may embark upon a snorkeling outing. The resort may offer free snorkel gear, including masks and flippers, so all you have to do is invite guests to your afternoon snorkeling party. Many resorts give out laminated guides to the different types of fish and coral that guests will see below the surface of the water, so pick up a batch of those cards for your guests' viewing and ID fun.

Also at a resort, your beach day could include free kayaking in solo or tandem kayaks, and guests say that they enjoy the easy, safe kayak outing in the non-surf waters on a resort's beach. If there is surf, or if kayak guides say this is not an area for beginners, skip this activity for your group's safety.

Boardwalk

Some boardwalks are home to multiple piers featuring many different types of rides from the family-friendly carousel to the thrill rides defying gravity. Your group's outing to a boardwalk will be best enjoyed when you stick together as a group, moving from pier to pier, riding the rides, playing the skill and chance games, perhaps even posing for old-time photos. Boardwalk-type foods such as funnel cakes, ice cream, fudge, and taffy are fabulous theme treats for your guests, and it's a nice touch if you, as host, bought a round of funnel cakes or ice cream cones for all of your guests.

Boating

Summertime fun on the water can take many forms, depending on where you are and what's offered there. You might charter a yacht to take you on a day's sail or evening dinner sail, hop aboard a catamaran, take a speedboat ride with a professional driver, or ride Jet Skis™ in a designated area with guides available to help your group's beginners operate their vehicles safely.

Money Mastery

Many public beaches charge for beach passes and require guests to wear wristbands or badges showing authorities that they have paid to be on the beach. Look for a public beach that does not charge a fee for beach entry.

A chartered boat ride might be that catamaran, and you'll also find unique craft such as glass-bottom boats and paddleboats, especially on lakes.

Check with your local park service to find out about boating companies in your area, as well as fees and requirements for boat rentals run by the park service itself.

Fishing and Crabbing

An offshoot of boating is the family fishing or crabbing trip. Some families have spent summers years ago sharing crabbing trips and may not have been able to keep up the tradition for years. So planning a group crabbing outing for a flotilla of motorboats is a thrilling return to those precious family memories.

Water Park

Modern water parks have become veritable theme parks, with higher, more adrenaline-filled waterslides, as well as tamer slides for the kids. With wave pools and other water features,

Watch Out!

Fishing trips are run by charter boat companies, but keep in mind that some boating outings go way out into deep water, and the waves may be too much for those who don't have sturdy sea legs. So unless your fishing trip is only for experienced fishermen and fisherwomen who know what to expect, it may be best to stick with a calmer water fishing experience, such as fishing off of a dock or from the edge of a lake. Be aware too that many municipalities require a permit for fishing of any kind, and you don't want to be in violation of the law-especially twenty times over with your guests fishing alongside you! Call the park system to ask where your group can fish without permits needed.

and cabanas and snack bars, your guests may be surprised to see that your local water park is exponentially more elaborate than the water parks they visited in their youth. Remember, water parks present safety challenges, so be sure that parents stay with their kids at all times.

Amusement Park

Thrill rides, kiddie rides, concerts, and shows—these are a big attraction at amusement parks big and small. Some groups whose weddings are located near the best-known amusement parks (think Disney, Universal Studios, Knott's Berry Farm) give guests the thrill of a lifetime when their trip to the wedding city includes a day spent at a dream destination amusement park even if they have to pay for their admission tickets.

As a possible money saver, call the amusement park to see if you can get discount group rates for your wedding group coming in for the day. And do say *wedding group*, since some parks treat bridal groups to special deals. Your local tourism bureau can also be a source of discounted group tickets, and don't forget that the guests' hotel concierge likely has a stack of two-for-one entrance tickets and other amusement park perks and coupons behind the desk. It's always smart to ask if you can use them.

Steal My Party Idea

"We surprised our guests who RSVP'd that they would come with us to Disneyworld with their own name-printed mouse ear hats, and we all posed for a photo at the castle!"–Julie, bride

Concerts in the Park

Your local tourism bureau is again the resource of choice to find out which nearby towns have fun, free concerts in the park. Your group can bring folding chairs and blankets, head to the local park's gazebo, and take in a concert featuring a symphony, bluegrass music, jazz artists, a cappella groups, show tune performers, even cover bands and kiddie concerts.

Movies in the Park

Towns with the space to do so often host movies in the park, with classic and current films projected either on buildings or on giant inflatable movie screens. Everyone sits in the open air, on chairs or on blankets, snack vendors abound, and the movie of the night plays on for free. Another twist on this is one that many guests love: a drive-in movie theater. While many have disappeared from the landscape, many still do exist. You can find one near you at DriveInMovie.com.

Fall

The fall season is, as mentioned, the start of football season, and for many guests that means taking in a game, tailgating, showing off their fan loyalty, or even just watching the big game on the big-screen TV, avoiding stadium prices and crowds and seeing every play in HD. There are also fall events that take advantage of the crisp, clean fall weather.

Football Game

You might take your group to a pro game, especially if you or someone in your group has season tickets. The energy in a stadium is palpable, and fall weather makes for a very enjoyable day if the stadium is open-air. In colder weather climates, stadiums are enclosed by a dome.

Steal My Party Idea

"We planned to watch the big game on television, but we set up a big tailgate party in the driveway where we grilled and had a keg, tossed the football around, sang game chants and cheers, and took plenty of pictures. At halftime, we went outside to play touch football, too. For an affordable party, it was really awesome."—Brent, groom

A less expensive twist on this plan is to go to the local high school's football game, which is a fabulous blast from the past if the bride or groom and their friends attended school at that local high school. They spent years going to weekly games, maybe playing on the football team or performing in the marching band or band front, cheering, or being a part of the pep squad. Now, the group's return to the high school brings a charge of energy and the chance for the group to reminisce and share their favorite high school moments.

Family Farm

In the fall months, a fabulous family farm might be just a short drive away, and there you'll find family-friendly activities such as a corn maze, a petting zoo, and hay rides. The farm's store offers wonderful shopping for guests who load up on homemade fruit breads, cider, and other snacks.

Orchard Picking

In early fall, it might be prime apple-picking season near you, or berry-picking, peach-picking, or any number of other harvesting opportunities. Check LocalHarvest.org to find a family farm near you, and the sites you visit will tell you what's in season, what's open for picking, and what else the farm has to offer on that weekend. Guests then spend the day in the fresh fall air, sharing a fruit-picking adventure in the orchards, and they get to take home their big bags of apples or berries, picked fresh from the trees, for making pies, tarts, or jams.

Watch Out!

This tour is best kept for an adults-only crowd for optimal enjoyment, and, of course, the presence of a designated driver is essential.

Winery Tour

Fall winery tours still include open-air dining, often set on a floral-strewn terrace or beneath arbors in the vineyard, and the tours also include guided walks through the winery's barrel rooms and other privileged areas. Your group can ask for a private tour and tasting of the winery's new vintages, served with a cheese course or a catered menu of appetizers, or desserts served with dessert wines and champagnes.

Alumni Events

Fall means back to school, and college towns welcome their students and their families back with weekends full of events, such as parties to celebrate the first home football game of the season, alumni picnics and cocktail parties, and other attractions. If the bride or groom attended college nearby or if the wedding takes place in the city of their alma mater—perhaps even on the grounds of the university itself—a call to the alumni office or a visit to the alumni page of the school's website will reveal a calendar of amazing events provided by the school.

Take the second step and check the community calendar for the university's town to learn about events that were smartly planned to take place during the same weekend. You'll find craft and arts festivals, fairs, pub tours, free concerts in the park, and many more activities your group can enjoy for free.

Winter

Winter fun includes playing in the snow, if there happens to be a fresh snowfall at the time of the wedding weekend. Since you can't predict these kinds of things, it's best to preface your invitation with "If Mother Nature gives us a winter wonderland," or something to that effect. Let guests know if they should bring their ski or skating gear, of course, and don't forget the post-play warmth by a fireplace, drinking hot cocoa or mulled wine or cider.

Location is key to this season's activities, since you might wish to host a sledding party at a home that has a great sloped yard and a fireplace, perhaps even an outdoor hot tub and outdoor fire pit. Some groups at winter destination weddings are already in a winter mecca that provides these dreamy gathering places outdoors, or at a fine ski lodge with an immense fireplace and a happening social scene.

Steal My Party Idea

"We knew that the Sundance Film Festival was taking place just an hour away from where we would be, so we scheduled a day to head over to Aspen for skiing, celebrity-spotting, shopping, and other exciting activities. It was a star-style party the bride and groom, and all the guests, loved."—Felicia, bridesmaid

Ice skating

When your group goes to an ice skating rink or roller skating ring, everyone gets the return to childhood memories, of group skate, backward skate, and couples' skate. Music plays and a deejay turns the atmosphere into a party. Experienced skaters get to show off their skills, and the little ones may perhaps take their first spin around a rink.

If your ice skating adventure has you on an open-air rink or on a frozen pond that the township has deemed safe for skating, your guests may get to enjoy skating while a light snowfall sends big, beautiful snowflakes to be caught on your tongue. After the chilly outdoor skate, everyone heads to your place or back to the hotel for a warm-up by the fireplace, hot drinks, and snacks.

Sledding and Tobogganing

Again, if you or someone you know has a fabulous sledding hill, you're all set. You'll find inexpensive toboggans at stores like Target and Toys"R"Us, and your party expense for providing a half dozen of these is still just a fraction of what other hosts may be paying for their upscale catered party.

Another form of this party is taking everyone to a local park to go sledding, joining the party atmosphere with all the people around you. Some wedding weekend event guests have found handsome strangers to flirt with, and kids quickly make friends with other children enjoying their winter fun at the park.

Steal My Party Idea

"I checked with a beauty salon near the guests' hotel and found out that they were having a winter beauty event, with skin treatments to guard against dry winter skin, hair deep conditioning treatments, manicures and pedicures, little snowflakes painted on little girls' nails, and more. I shared the link with the bride and all of her friends, and we went there the day after the wedding for some VIP beauty treatments specific to winter weather beauty needs. And they served us mulled wine and eggnog with Christmas cookies. It was too much fun."

—Melanie, bridesmaid

Tree-Lighting Event

If your party takes place before the Christmas holidays, perhaps even during Thanksgiving weekend when some townships hold their Christmas kickoff parades culminating in a tree-lighting ceremony, take your group to the town center to join in the fun of a festive celebration. The parade itself gets everyone into the holiday spirit, and when you buy a round of coffee or hot chocolate, your event is a fun one.

Ski Resort Events

In addition to the winter festivals held at ski resorts, you'll also find an array of events hosted by the ski resort you may be staying at, or may be staying close to. These events include cognac tastings at the hotel, nighttime skiing with everyone carrying glow sticks, cocktail parties and nightclub theme nights for dancing and drinking from the ice luge.

Talk to friends who frequent nearby ski resorts to find out which resorts have the best attractions available to non-guests, and check the websites for each resort or hotel to learn its calendars of activities.

CHAPTER 18

 **Cultural Events**

If your circle enjoys the arts, plan an outing to take in a cultural event. This is one event category that you might think the parents claim as their own, taking their friends and colleagues to the theater as their group outing, but it's quickly becoming a universal pastime. Don't assume that by *cultural event* I mean only the opera or the ballet. Any type of arts performance or exhibit is an option here, and guests of all ages enjoy a great concert, art showing, or trip to a museum.

In this chapter, you'll explore some of the most popular styles of cultural events, learn how to find scheduled performances and attractions near you, and plan your group outing in inspiring style.

Types of Events

The arts are alive and well—music, dance, comedy, performance art. Just take a look at the schedule for your local community theater and city theaters and you'll discover an impressive list of performances that your group can take in. I looked at my own local theater and found the following dance performances:

Dance, Music, and Comedy

> ➤ Savion Glover

> ➤ New Jersey Ballet performing *Cinderella* (and tickets were just $12 apiece!)

- ➤ New Jersey Ballet performing *Sleeping Beauty*

- ➤ Tango Buenos Aires

- ➤ Celtic Fire

- ➤ Russian National Ballet

Then I looked for jazz performances and found:

- ➤ George Winston

- ➤ Dukes of Dixieland

For musicals I found:

- ➤ *Legally Blonde: The Musical*

- ➤ *All Shook Up: The Elvis Tribute*

- ➤ *Cats*

In the classical genre I found:

- ➤ New Jersey Symphony Orchestra performing *Arabian Nights* music

- ➤ New Jersey Symphony Orchestra performing Spanish Flair music

- ➤ Philharmonic of Poland

- ➤ Choir of the Pope's Diocese of Rome

That's right: the Pope's choir coming right here to New Jersey, which proves you never know who's coming to your area and how inexpensive tickets can be.

For comedy, I had the choice of seeing the following:

- ➤ Lily Tomlin

- ➤ Wanda Sykes

- ➤ Lewis Black

- ➤ Kevin Smith

- ➤ Bill Cosby

- ➤ *One-Man Star Wars Trilogy*, a show in which one actor takes on every role in the film.

Those were just the comedians coming to my local community theater in the current year. I mention them all just to give you a taste of the range of arts performances available and to get you thinking about what your group might enjoy most. Your friends might love an evening with Kevin Smith, while other guests would rather join the group going to the

3 pm ballet production of *Cinderella*. Keep in mind, theaters often have three or four different performances scheduled for a single extended weekend of Thursday through Sunday, so you may find arts opportunities in the wedding weekend block that would be perfect for your guests.

Museums

For just a small entry fee, sometimes for no admission price at all, your group can take in a fascinating exhibit at a nearby museum. The Museum of Natural History in New York City, for instance, offers a butterfly-filled biodome featuring thousands upon thousands of beautiful, colorful butterflies in a natural habitat filled with trees and flowering plants. You walk through the exhibit, and, if you're lucky, a butterfly will land on you. It's said to be good luck if one does.

Steal My Party Idea

"It's amazing how you have no idea what's going on at the local museums! A friend told me that the museum a few towns away had a brand-new, state-of-the-art planetarium, so we arranged for our group to visit there and look through its super-powered telescopes to see distant planets and galaxies. Everyone said they loved it!"—Lia, bridesmaid

Other exhibits your group may love include collections of archaeology finds, historical costumes, Hollywood props, and dinosaurs. Your group tours the museum and then goes for lunch as the perfect day-after outing.

Finding Cultural Events

To attend these shows and get group tickets at a discounted rate, you have to have plenty of advance notice of scheduled performances. So get on the mailing list for all of the community theaters in your area. You'll be surprised to see that even the so-called little theaters attract big-name entertainers and impressive musical groups. You'll get ticket advisories via e-mail and will be among the first to know when a favorite artist is coming to town.

Visit the websites for your regional magazines, where you'll find community calendars listing the various cultural performances scheduled for the next few months. At NewJerseyMonthly.com, for instance, I discovered that the bride and groom's favorite comedian was slated to perform at an Atlantic City casino during the wedding weekend, so we quickly snagged tickets and surprised the happy couple with their wedding weekend event that happened to fall two nights before their wedding.

Many communities now have their own Facebook pages, and they announce their upcoming cultural events to boost tourism, so sign on there or view their public wall every now and then, and remember that posters announcing arts events spring up at various establishments around town. These include:

➤ Coffee shops

➤ Libraries

➤ Bakeries

➤ Community centers

Dance academies and universities are hotbeds of performance information, so check in there as well, even going to the music department at the local college to see what's posted on the bulletin board. Not everything gets onto a college website, so the in-person discovery method sometimes reveals the most wonderful cultural opportunities.

Finally, check the township website, where arts events are also listed and where you can find a URL for the event to include in your invitations.

Planning Tips

If an event would attract lots of out-of-town guests such as college friends coming in from miles away, give these people months of advance notice—which is very possible when a community theater posts their calendar of events for the year. Some may wish to arrange their travel and lodging schedule to let them stay the extra day in order to join your group at that concert or comedy show. This advice also applies to local friends whose schedules fill up quickly. They'll appreciate the advance notice and will create the time to join your group on this fun outing.

Share the details of the event in your invitations. A link to the theater's or museum's page will entice guests with glowing descriptions of the performance or exhibit, and everyone can easily see that the *Cinderella* performance is just $12.

Money Mastery

Ask the establishment how many tickets constitute a group rate, and if you have eight people in your group but the minimum is ten tickets, buy the ten tickets and get the discount. You can then give the two extra tickets to a special guest, or just have them handy for the inevitable guest who expresses interest after the RSVP date. You can also sell these tickets for face value at work. For a great show, they won't go to waste.

That brings up the money issue. Decide before you say a word about this event whether or not you, as host or together with co-hosts, will pay for the group's tickets, or if you'll do your etiquette-friendly part by letting guests know in the invitation that you can arrange for discounted tickets as part of a group. Your research (calling the theater) has revealed that group tickets to *Cinderella* would cost just $8 apiece, and you share this information with your RSVP details of where to contact you, how to send payment, and the absolute drop-dead latest date when people can buy their tickets.

Transportation

For the vast majority of wedding weekend hosts, the plan is for everyone to drive to the theater, museum, or other location where the performance will take place. Volunteers are recruited to drive, guests are picked up at their hotel (even if they rented cars since they may be charged for their extra mileage), and the group ride to the event becomes part of the fun. Delia, a bridesmaid, says, "We used car-painting soap to decorate our car windows, announcing that we're off to see the ballet! It was such a different message, we saw so many people on the road appreciating it and pointing us out to their kids! So we were a traveling advertisement for the arts!"

Another popular transportation option for groups of fourteen or fewer is to rent a limousine, splitting the charge for the rides there and back. A $150 limo ride split seven ways is just a little more than $20 per couple, which is a great deal considering no one would have to pay tolls and parking garage fees. And you'd get to travel in style, enjoying a bottle of wine or champagne as you head to the concert, plus additional drinks on the way home.

Watch Out!

When you're shopping around for limousine or party bus rentals, if you haven't done so before, check the package and contract carefully for financial-impact charges like an automatic 18 percent gratuity—so you don't double-tip at the end of the night—and be very aware of the end time for your event so that you don't get charged a fortune for overtime. Rental vehicles often start the clock when they leave their lot, so ask the agency how much time you lose from your allotted hours due to the car's travel to and from your location.

If your event will be attended by a group of more than fifteen people, look into renting a party bus. Today's upscale models have leather seats, plasma TVs, sound systems, and mood lighting; they create a party on wheels. It could be the perfect treat for the couple and the guests, a worry-free ride (with cocktails!) in VIP style to the concert of the year. Again, everyone can split the cost of the party bus, and with more people attending, that $20 fee could still be in play. Hosts who worry about asking guests to split the lofty price of a party bus solve their dilemma by asking guests to contribute a bit less than the full split price. For instance, let's say a couple's share for a ride in the party bus would be $35. The host can ask them for $25 per couple, which pays for most of the expense and is still a very fair price for the experience and the perks. The host picks up the rest.

Add-On Expenses

Think about the timing of this arts event. If it's an 8 pm performance, will you include dinner before the show in this outing? If it's a 3 pm arts festival, will you treat everyone to dinner when your group is still at the festival at 6 pm. It's important to think through this part of your plan so you don't wind up on the spot, feeling obligated to buy twenty people dinner since they're all looking at you like they expected you to.

Another add-on for arts events is the keepsake. You don't have to buy concert T-shirts for everyone. Guests can buy their own items.

Parking fees for your volunteer drivers is one item that nice for you, the host, to pay for. They're doing you a favor by driving, and they might not expect that three hours in a parking garage near the theater is going to cost them $20. Let all of your drivers know that you'll pick up that expense for them. It's just a nice thing to do, and good etiquette is the most impressive art form.

CHAPTER 19

For Families with Kids

In This Chapter

➤ Activities on the town

➤ Activities at the hotel

➤ Favors and other goodies

So many brides and grooms are allowing their wedding guests to bring their children to the wedding celebrations. And even if kids aren't invited to an adults-only reception, parents might bring their kids with them on the trip to the wedding location, with a sitter looking after the kids during the official wedding events. This means the entire wedding group has lots of kids with them, and since weddings are reunions between friends and family members who haven't seen each other in years, guests want the chance to introduce everyone to their new babies, toddlers, and adorable tweens. Other guests want to see the kids. Parents want to keep their kids entertained, and kids want to *be* entertained. And the trend of planning kid-centric wedding weekend activities is born.

This chapter will inspire you with a collection of the most popular kid-pleasing, parent-approved activities. Parents, for the most part, don't want to ship their kids off to the hotel's kiddie camp and go off to do their own thing. They want their kids to play with their friends' kids, and they want to be nearby to share in the smiles and play right alongside them. You'll find the perfect activities here, and perhaps be inspired to look into other activities.

Let's get going . . .

Off-Site Activities

While we are going to look at the kids' activities and amenities offered at the hotel where the guests are staying—since on-site fun makes things a bit easier for all—let's start with a range of activities you'll have to drive to. Parents and their kids meet in the hotel lobby at a set time to be shuttled to the chosen locale.

Game Center

Even with the proliferation of game systems like the Wii, PlayStation, and Xbox, kids still want to go to gaming centers that offer arcade games, laser tag, go-karts, climbing walls, and other high-energy games. Parents love it, too, since they can play alongside their kids—not always possible with a home gaming console—and show off their skills to their children and their friends. For this reason, the game center is the number one off-site destination for wedding weekend events focused on kids.

Another reason game centers are popular is because they accommodate kids of all ages, which is a boon when you have kids as young as three in your group and as old as sixteen. A game center provides games and activities for many different ages, including an easier climbing wall designed for tiny bodies and little feet.

Money Mastery

Admission tickets to game centers aren't that expensive, but the tokens necessary to play as well as special tickets for laser tag and go-karts add up to a sizeable cost. If you're paying for all as host, or if the parental guests will be paying, save yourselves a fortune by collecting coupons for the game center. You'll find these in Sunday paper coupon inserts, Valpak and other local coupon offerings, Coupons.com, and through simple Google searches. The game center's own website will likely have coupon offers, and—here's the big one—when you and friends sign onto the game center's mailing list, you'll get coupons in the mail or via e-mail that can give you one hundred free tokens, two-for-one entry, and other money-saving perks. Collect your own, and ask your network of parent friends if they have any coupons they won't be using anytime soon and would be willing to give you or trade.

Bowling

The number two ranking kids' activity is bowling, with the little ones given lanes lined with bumpers, preventing frustration and making it possible for them to knock down some pins. Parents bowling on bumper lanes also may top their high scores, and kids love having the entire group on their lane cheering for them even if they knock down just one pin.

With a snack bar menu of pizzas and fries, pitchers of soda, desserts you bring from home, party music piped throughout the place, and even laser light shows and other effects, the bowling alley is a top draw for wedding weekend event groups filled with kids of all ages.

Skate Park

With advance notice given, kids can bring their skateboards, skates, helmets, and pads to the new skate park located in your town. Especially if kids don't have a skate park—with its concrete slopes and trick bars—near them, they'll love the chance to pretend with the other kids that they're at the X Games, showing off their skills.

Playground

Little ones can play on the slide or the swings, older ones can tackle the obstacle course, and parents can marvel at how far playgrounds have come in their design and safety standards since they were kids. An afternoon spent at the playground lets kids run off their pent-up energy with no organized activity in sight. They're free to play basketball with the ball you've brought along, swing from ropes and bars, jump, and play.

Steal My Party Idea

"Since we had several generations attending the wedding, we turned our playground visit into a fun activity in which the grandparent generation taught the little ones how to play the games they had played—like hopscotch or jacks—and the little ones showed the grandparents the games they play."—Sarah, bride

Parents can play as well, or just sit in the shade keeping an eye on all of the playground fun as a fantastic morning, afternoon, or evening planned event.

Movies

Forget about trying to find a family movie that no one has seen yet. Just plan an outing to the local multiplex to see the newest Pixar movie or the newest film starring the kids' favorite actor at. In daytime, you'll get the matinee rate, coupons may be available, and group discounts are often yours for the asking. The newest attraction at many movie theaters is a special late morning showing that welcomes parents with babies who are likely to cry, small children who are likely to talk or run around—in short, a welcoming atmosphere for those who previously had to avoid movie theaters due to their kids' noise and activity levels. Now, with everyone toting their noisy kids along, it's an environment of understanding and tolerance, and you get to see a movie. This could be the perfect movie showing for your circle of parents with very young kids.

Prevent stress by making it a must for parents to attend this movie with their kids, not hand the little ones off to you while they lie by the pool drinking margaritas. No, this isn't a daycare outing. It's a group event for parents with kids, and parents must attend. You'll word it in your invitations like this:

> Parents and children ages zero to sixteen are invited
> to join us at the multiplex
> for the 11 am showing of *Toy Story 12*!
> Parents MUST accompany their children!
> Discount rates are $6 for adults and $4 for kids.

To avoid further aggravation, don't e-mail all the parents to ask which movie their kids would like to see. What you'll get are dozens of e-mails turning into a swirling vortex of "my kid saw this" or "my kid wants to see this" or "my kid can handle seeing an R-rated movie." That's right, some parents might be the type to bring the kids along to a movie the parents want to see. And they may be nervy enough to try to sway your group movie plans to a film choice that's a bit saucy for the little ones. It's perfectly find to e-mail back with your decision of "no, the group is going to see *Toy Story 12*, and we've arranged for a discount. But thanks for the suggestion." No need to finish that sentence with any judgment about that particular suggestion!

If you'll be picking up the cost of movie tickets, as announced in your invitations, parents will pick up the costs of the food and drink their kids want to enjoy. You can make this clear in your invitations with "Visit the website of the movie theater to see the snack bar prices for your kids' popcorn, candy, and soda treats." Message clear.

Theater

The local community theater likely has a wide range of kid-friendly arts on its performance calendar, and the wedding weekend might be the very same weekend when the theater is hosting a performance of *The Nutcracker* or the kid-mesmerizing Pilobolus dance art act, even a kids' magician, puppet show, kid-friendly musical, or cultural dance group that will keep kids captivated with the color, sound, and movement.

Check the theater calendar to see what's slated during your pockets of available time—most likely the early afternoon on the day after the wedding—and your group might be lucky enough to cap off a winter wedding weekend with the kids' very first *Nutcracker* experience. No one ever forgets their first time.

Museum

Your region may be home to a kids' museum or kids' science center with hands-on educational displays, fascinating sites, even performances and guided tours. If an intriguing museum is within driving distance, lead your group of parents, grandparents, and kids for an afternoon spent exploring the many different facets of the museum.

What you might find, as many hosts do, is that your region is home to many more museums than you first expected. From historical museums, to art museums, early trade and craft museums, and more, the arts council of your town—as well as the regional magazine or website's calendar—will inform you of incoming exhibits that you can prebook at a discount.

Festivals

Again, festivals are a gold mine for kids' activities, with all of the sights, sounds, smells, and tastes enrapturing the little ones. Kids get to eat big baked pretzels, cotton candy, ice cream, hot dogs, and more, and artists might paint flowers or a Spider-Man design on the kids' cheeks.

Free concerts welcome kids to come right up front and dance to the delight of the crowd, and some festivals offer the kiddie crowd-pleasing pony rides and petting zoos that some little ones might not have ever experienced before.

Shop Here!

Go to the museum's website and look into becoming a member or patron of the museum. It often costs less than $20, earns you discount rates on entry fees and shopping in the gift shop, and members are often welcome to reserve the museum for their special events, parties—even weddings! If you're a party hosts who has her own wedding coming up, perhaps your membership at the museum will net you big savings and a spectacular setting for your own welcome cocktail party, rehearsal dinner, or wedding itself!

Craft Center

At a crafting party, parents accompany their kids to an arts-based store with a certain theme. It might be a jewelry-making kids' party place, or a ceramics studio. In recent years, a number of ultra-creative art studios have popped up in large and small towns across the country as more people join the ranks of the entrepreneurs, running their own businesses or franchises of kiddie activity centers. Parents who don't want the chaos of the gaming center prefer the organized creativity of a kids' art center that hosts kiddie parties.

Here are just some of the kids' craft party stores you'll find to consider for your wedding weekend activity for families with kids:

➤ Ceramics with kids painting a wall tile or light switch wall plate

➤ Pottery with kids working a small low-powered potting wheel to make a bud vase

➤ Jewelry making or beading

➤ Cupcake decorating

➤ Cookie decorating

➤ Sand art

At resorts, for a destination wedding, the arts and crafts gurus employed by the resort can lead your group in a range of projects from flower pressing to taking molds of animal prints left in the sand, to making shadow boxes filled with sand dollars and starfish and shells. Call the concierge desk of the resort hotel to find out about craft events for children in the age demographic of your group. Tweens won't want to glue macaroni to an ashtray, so match your craft choice to the kids' ages well, with the parents' help if you don't have children of your own.

On-Site Activities

Next up is the kid-friendly activity that takes place right at the hotel where the guests are staying; activities that take place at your home (or someone else's home) also qualify for this category, keeping the party at a convenient and comfortable location.

Watch Out!

You might have the nicest in-ground pool among your circle of friends, and thus the party could be at your place. Just keep in mind that a kids' pool party does present certain risks, so make sure your home insurance policy has adequate coverage for any injuries that occur on your property.

Hotel Activities

The hotel or resort will likely have a schedule of events for kids, and those may include treasure hunts, volleyball parties, and other activities that are designed for kids of all ages. All you have to do is provide parents with the details of the activity, set up a meeting time, and your easy, free weekend activity comes together easily and is led by the resort's trained staff.

Swim Party

Whether it's in the hotel's pool or in your own backyard pool, the kids' swim party is prime for free-time play, without any planned activities such as limbo competitions or diving for pennies. Kids would rather do their own thing, run wild, create their own water games, race each other all on their own without anyone telling them how to do anything.

A kids' pool party naturally occurs with a barbecue taking place poolside, or the kids can get burgers and pizza from the hotel snack bar right by the pool. Again, it's up to you if you want to buy a round of burgers and sodas, then leave any secondary snack bar drinks or menu orders up to the kids' parents, or if you want to cover the entire kids' party snack tab.

Game Day

This one takes place at a private home, where a big-screen HDTV, surround sound system, a top-shelf game system, and lots of room create the perfect gaming "cave" for the kids to play in. This hi-tech game night can have kids plugging in to battle each other in the newest must-have video game. You serve kid-friendly snacks or order pizzas, or let the kids top their own personal pizzas with their choices of toppings.

If you don't have access to a top-of-the-line video game system, kids and parents can join in for rounds of retro games. From your basement comes the original Battleship, the original Connect 4, the original Hungry, Hungry Hippo, and other games. Little ones might build with Lincoln Logs as their parents play right along with them. Producing retro toys and games creates a fun twist to the usual kids' game party.

Movie Night

Movies shown at home can be noisy, chaotic activities, especially if kids are sugared up and they're not in a public place where they have to behave. So don't go crazy buying the latest DVD releases. Whatever you have or can borrow will only be partially watched by a roomful of hyper kids anyway, and they'll still love it.

Theme Party

Parents love to throw creatively themed parties such as princess parties and cowboy- or pirate-themed parties for their kids. Whether or not you have children of your own, you might choose to plan the same type of fun theme party for the kids and their parents—no birthday girl or boy required. Everyone just dresses up in costume, the décor, games, and even the food fits the chosen theme, and your prowess as a party planner is on full display.

Here are the top kids' party themes at the time of this book's writing:

➤ *Harry Potter*

➤ *Twilight*

➤ *Hannah Montana*

➤ *Alice in Wonderland*

➤ Barbie

➤ Superhero

➤ Pirate

➤ Bugs—ladybug, butterfly, bumblebee—kids dress up like their favorite bug; a good chance for parents to get another use out of a child's Halloween costume. The cake is in the shape of the bug, and the activity is collecting gummi worms in the yard.

➤ Dalmatian—the theme is actually black and white, and kids can come dressed up in black-and-white clothes or go all out with a dalmation hat or costume, dress like a penguin or other black-and-white outfitting. Your décor, cake, invitations—everything is black and white!

➤ Disney characters

➤ Fairies

➤ Tea party

➤ Luau

➤ Race car driving—kids wear their favorite race car driver's number, and they can play race car video games to determine who's the champion.

➤ Sports

➤ *Star Wars*

➤ *Toy Story*

➤ *Wizard of Oz*

➤ Winter Wizards—just a cute way of getting kids to wear winter-white shirts, put on ice-blue and silver butterfly wings and ice-blue toy tiaras, etc., to become winter wizards for your magical winter kids' party. Serve Italian ice in wintry white, blue, or red and kids will love it. Add in sledding, snowball throwing, and other fun in the snow element, and this party is a kids' dream come true.

Favors and Other Details

Are favors necessary at these kid-centric parties? Isn't it enough just to give the kids a great experience, plus fantastic foods and treats? Yes, you can say that it is, and you can skip the expense and effort of creating and distributing goodie bags if you wish. Or, you can decide to create them—for both the kids *and* the parents.

Just match the favors or goodie bags to the party's theme. If it's a pool party, the favors can be funky sunglasses from the dollar store, kids' colored sunscreen tubes, or packs of water balloons. If it's a tea party, the girls' goodie bags can have packets of tea cakes or truffles, and the parents' goodie bags can have tins or packets of flavored teas.

One item that kids love is the single-use camera, which you can find in white or pink floral designs for the girls, perhaps perfect for that tea party, Barbie party, or other themed get-together. For boys, one-time-use cameras come in solid colors of blue, purple, even black. At a pool party, the single-use camera can be an underwater camera that kids can use in and around the pool. No worries about a camera getting soaked and ruined.

Are sleepovers a good idea for kids' parties? You might think it would be a blast for the kids, and give the parents a romantic evening alone together, but if you're not an experienced parent, you may find yourself dealing with lots of chaos and perhaps even a ride back to the hotel with a child who's become sick from all of that sugary food you fed him during the party. Stay on the safe side and skip the idea of sleepovers for this particular weekend. There's too much on the line. Keep the kids' event short and sweet, and it'll be a big success.

Etiquette Friendly

Be sure to honor the bride and groom's scheduled events for the entirety of the weekend. If, for instance, the bride and groom have planned an event for 4 pm the day after the wedding, be sure to close down your kids' party no later than 2 pm so everyone has time to get back to the hotel, shower, change, and be ready to attend the wedding couple's event. It would be a terrible thing if you lost track of time at your kid's party and the guests were late getting to the bride and groom's event.

CHAPTER 20

Big-Ticket Outings

In This Chapter

➤ Extravagant outings

➤ The guest list

➤ Preparing for your big-ticket event

Brides and grooms often give generous thank-you gifts to their parents who paid for their weddings, and the new trend is to make this gift a big-ticket experience during the wedding weekend. We're seeing couples getting VIP tickets to see their parents' favorite performers in concert, and the couple and a handful of special guests get to go along as well. "We were able to get six tickets to Barbra Streisand's concert, which we knew both sets of parents would *love*. Tenth row, too. So we surprised them with the tickets, and we all went to the concert two nights before the wedding. Our moms were in tears!" says Melinda, a recent bride.

Another trend is brides and grooms surprising each other with big-ticket events to share with a small circle of friends or family members during the wedding weekend.

If you haven't just won the Mega Millions, your budget is going to dictate which big-ticket event you can plan, as well as who will join you, and this chapter suggests some of the different types of top-tier events you might plan, and how best to plan them.

Types of Big-Ticket Outings

The first category is the concert of the summer, that sold-out show that everyone wants to see. It might be a solo concert by a top-name artist or one of those group concerts put on by the *American Idol* finalists, which makes for great fun when your circle of friends are rabid fans of the show. Similarly to the *AI* concert is the tour of finalists from a dance competition such as *Dancing with the Stars* or another similar show.

Money Mastery

Check the website for your local sports team to see if you can buy discounted tickets or blocks of face-value tickets through that site. Season ticket-holders are often required to sell the tickets they can't use through the NFL teams' online ticket exchange system, and you may be best protected by going through this official channel. You don't want to PayPal someone $300 for tickets based on a dicey website ad and find out that the person is a scammer, your money lost. Always practice smart ticket purchasing through a trusted website.

Weddings that take place in casino meccas such as Las Vegas are ripe for these big-ticket shows, with your guests being treated to an in-residence superstar's performance. "We asked our wedding coordinator at Caesar's if we could get tickets to Bette Midler's show, and they gave four tickets to us at a discount price, as a thanks for being a destination wedding couple!" says Charlotte, a recent bride. Don't forget that casinos have piles of complimentary tickets to all kinds of shows, so that big-ticket concert experience is not always going to be a big-ticket expense.

Another big-ticket experience is a theater production. Some Broadway plays and touring Broadway productions can be seen for upward of $75 per ticket—sometimes more—and hosts consider it their gift to the wedding couple to bring them and their guests to see the hottest musical or their favorite megawatt actor in his or her Broadway performance.

Sporting events too qualify for big-ticket outings, even for a non-playoff game. At some stadiums even the nosebleed seats cost a pretty penny, but it's worth every penny to bring the bride and groom and their guests to experience the energy and thrill of seeing their favorite NFL team playing another favorite NFL team or rival team. Since most games take place at 1 pm, 4 pm, or 8 pm on a Sunday, this often makes for the perfect timing for a big-ticket event for football fans. And, of course, the same goes for baseball, basketball, or any other sporting event.

Tapping again into cultural events, your big-ticket event of choice might be to the opera or the ballet, or even to an elite fundraising dinner attended by celebrities and sports megastars. Check the charity events listings on your region's community calendars, and you might be dressed up, sipping champagne, snacking on dishes prepared by celebrity chefs, reviewing valuable silent auction items, and mingling with the glitterati and celebrities you've always admired. And your big tickets benefit a worthy cause.

Who's Invited?

Since we're talking about very expensive tickets, this category is most often reserved just for the smallest VIP circle. The bride and groom may attend, but they might also depart for their honeymoon the day after the wedding. This big-ticket event might be their parents' event to attend without them. The ideal thank-you gift and a well-deserved high-life experience after giving the couple the wedding of their dreams.

Brides and grooms often don't want to miss out on a big-ticket event, so count them on the guest list, and think about the following people as you plan:

> ➤ Both sets of parents. This is an important etiquette issue, since the bride and groom don't want to start off married life with the family diplomacy nightmare of perceived favoritism of her parents over his parents, or vice versa. Even if the bride's parents paid for the majority of the wedding, it would be best to include all parents in a group event.

> ➤ The bride's and groom's siblings and their partners.

> ➤ The entire bridal party and their guests. This one has a significant etiquette quotient to it. It would be bad etiquette to invite just some of the bridal party members, such as the maid of honor and best man, leaving the others out. It might seem like a great way to thank the top-ranked bridal party members for their help with the wedding, but it would slight all the others who also gave their time and money to participate in the wedding plans. Consider the entire bridal party a bloc of guests. Don't handpick those you feel are most deserving.

> ➤ Entire destination wedding guest lists. Again, you can't bring some and not others to a pricy performance or dinner at a five-star celebrity restaurant, so go all-inclusive for this already small group.

Watch Out!

The guest list issue can get tricky, so consult with the bride and groom for their input—if it's not a surprise event. They may decide it's too much of a diplomacy nightmare to treat their VIP list of closest friends to such an event, since word would inevitably get out among other friends and they'd be left with dramas and rifts in their relationships. When a couple has a tricky social circle and strong feelings against VIP lists, it may be better to choose a different style of wedding weekend event. You never want your brilliant idea for a big-ticket event to turn into a nightmare for the bride and groom before, during, or after their big day.

Planning Tips

Big-ticket events become most-loved experiences, so design the outing to have a great beginning, middle, and end. For instance, a limousine ride to the concert allows you a celebrity-style ride and delivers you right to the front gates at the VIP entrance.

A preshow dinner is likely to be part of the package, so choose a wonderful restaurant for your guests to enjoy. Allow more than two hours for your dining adventure, since you may run into service delays on a busy theater night, and you'll want to enjoy a nice, leisurely dinner without any pressure to get to the show on time.

If your big-ticket event is a sports game, plan an elaborate tailgate party with décor, a tablecloth sporting the team's colors, and a fabulous menu that goes beyond hot dogs and hamburgers. Tailgate aficionados line up catered trays such as sausage, peppers, and onions, filet mignon, bourbon-soaked ribs, even lobster tails or king crab legs. Bring plenty of chairs for your guests to use and table seating for easier enjoyment of your luscious meal.

Send your VIP guests print invitations designed to reflect the theme of the big-ticket event, such as design the cover of the invitation to look like the playbill for the Broadway play you'll be seeing, or send a square invitation bearing the image of the singer's latest album on the front cover. A well-designed print invitation conveys a more impressive tone than an e-invitation, and hosts of this type of party say they love to add extra sparkle to these invitations, such as affixing stick-on crystals to convey the marquee lights of Broadway or the lights on the Vegas strip.

Sporting event invitations, even for ultra-expensive top-tier events like playoff games, can be sent via Evite if you wish, since that site has a great variety of football-themed invitations. You'll just up the excitement factor with your wording:

> "Join us at the Dolphins game!
> Joshua scored tickets for our VIPs,
> and we're stadium bound on Sunday, September 16th
> We leave at 9 am, and we have a tailgate party planned
> you'll never forget!"

And it's also a must to convey in your invitation the dress code for your big-ticket event. While some people may go to Broadway plays in jeans and sweaters, your plans to have dinner at Trump Tower means that everyone has to dress up. Here's wording that works:

> "Since we'll be going to dinner at the famous Trump Tower
> prior to the show,
> please honor Mr. Trump's dress code:
> suits and dresses are mandatory for guests of the restaurant."

Finally, if anyone helps you land your big tickets, such as the person with the season tickets to the pro sports team, or someone who alerted you to the upcoming concert, send them a big thank-you gift after the wedding weekend—even if they were there to share it with you. It might not have happened without them, and it's a wonderful touch of class to thank them for playing such a big part in that fantastic experience that everyone loved so much.

CHAPTER 21

Pampering and Spa

In This Chapter

➤ The range of party styles

➤ Treatment Options

➤ Getting ready for pampering

At your pampering and spa party, the ladies get together to sit back, relax, and enjoy pampering spa treatments. This chapter will help you select the style of pampering party that best suits your guest list and budget, with your location's spa offerings up for your consideration. For instance, if you're attending a destination wedding, the resort where everyone is staying likely has an amazing spa featuring exotic treatments with massage tables looking out over the clear blue ocean, or perhaps even set on the beach. As the event host, you might simply book a group visit to the resort's spa, with your guests invited to select the type of treatment they'd most enjoy. It could be a simple manicure, a lotus flower foot soak and pedicure, or an indulgent aloe body wrap or mud bath.

If you're not at a destination wedding resort, you'll have to arrange for spa treatments for your chosen circle of guests, and there are equally upscale ways to plan them. This chapter leads you through your search and arrangement of a ladies' spa party that makes this wedding weekend stand out for them as among the best they'll ever experience.

Read on to discover the newest trends in spa party styles, locations, and treatments, as well as the essential planning ideas that add extra-special details to your event.

Party Styles

We'll begin with the truly exorbitant and upscale party styles for those with big budgets and celebrity-style party-hosting acumen, and we'll progress through an array of additional spa party styles to help you zero in on the one that your guest circle would most enjoy and that suits your budget comfortably.

The Five-Star Hotel Spa Party

If the wedding takes place at a five-star hotel or casino, you will likely find an equally upscale spa right on the property. With stunning décor, enormous floral arrangements in their lobbies, complimentary glasses of Cristal for all, and $200 spa treatments on the menu, this is an experience that many brides choose for just their bridal party members and the mothers. It could, after all, easily cost more than the wedding itself if they were to host all out-of-town guests for a morning spent at the spa, with each guest getting a $200 facial.

Steal My Party Idea

"Since my parents put so much time and money into planning my wedding, I planned this event just for my mother and me to enjoy on our own, for the VIP experience she deserves, and some quiet mother-daughter time the day before the wedding."—Sheila, bride

This type of big-money spa experience is often planned as a duo experience, with many brides and grooms sharing the upscale lavishness of it. Some grooms even plan this spa visit as a surprise for their brides, stealing them away from the hectic last-minute wedding plans for a rejuvenating spa visit that counts as a wedding gift to the bride. Some grooms plan this as gift number one for their brides! And some brides plan this as a gift to their grooms, booking a romantic on-the-beach massage at sunrise, just for them.

The Salon Party

Today's ingenious beauty salons and spas know that the wedding realm is big business, so they now offer spa parties for bridal groups, closing their doors to others and offering a private party just for the bride and her circle of friends. They set up a lavish buffet and champagne bar, and the bride and her friends walk around in luxurious spa robes and slippers, taking turns getting facials and paraffin treatments, massages and wraps, manicures and pedicures, and eyebrow shapings. Some bridal groups book limousines to take them to and from the salon, giving all a celebrity-style VIP party experience.

The Poolside Spa Party

A friend who has a gorgeous in-ground pool with jaw-dropping landscaping, an outdoor sound system, a waterfall, hot tub, koi pond, and other dreamy elements you might see on shows like *The Real Housewives of Beverly Hills* can offer to have you host your poolside spa party at their place—or if this is your property I've just described, your home is where the party is.

You'll book a team of massage therapists, manicurists, and other beauty experts, in addition to a caterer and servers, bartenders, and even provide valet parking out front for this elite-style poolside spa party, and the ladies can lounge poolside as they enjoy the gourmet fare and champagne drinks brought to them by smiling servers.

At-Home Spa Party

Without a pool in your yard, you can arrange this spa party to take place in your home, with your guests in those spa robes sipping champagne, but with treatment areas set up in each of your bedrooms that have been cleaned and decorated with floral accent pieces and candles to create the perfect relaxing environments for massages and facials.

Your local spa manager can arrange for its employees to work your party on an evening after they end their work day at the spa, ensuring you professional treatment and the best-quality products and equipment available. Consider as one option the popularity of hot stone massages. The spa's hot stone massage specialist can bring her hot stone cooker and portable warming massage table to your home to give your guests an authentic massage of that nature.

The DIY At-Home Spa Party

It's the same as the at-home spa party, with your guests in spa robes and sipping their champagne or wine, but there are no beauty experts at your place because this is a DIY beauty treatment party. You create a nail polish bar featuring new bottles of nail polish found at your local discount beauty supply company in a range of colors from pastel to bright, as well as French manicure bottle duos, and everyone gathers at the tablecloth-covered kitchen table to do her own nails.

Money Mastery

Ask the bride's wedding coordinator to suggest spa service companies that conduct this type of party, as well as caterers and especially great-quality rental agencies where you can get celebrity-style lounging couches that are the new, hot must-have furniture at outdoor parties. An events coordinator knows the best companies and may be able to broker you a fine discount. You, after all, may be her future bridal client!

Watch Out!

Always book professionals found through a spa, since their experts must be licensed and insured. Never look online for independent spa practitioners whose equipment may be outdated and unsafe and whose methods may be disappointing at the very least.

Steal My Party Idea

"I planned a girls' pajama party that our teen guests could enjoy too, and asked everyone to bring or wear their cutest pajamas. We did each other's nails, danced to 80s music, and prank-called the groom while we drank milkshakes."—Anne, bride

A basket of trial-sized scented lotions awaits the group over at your foot station, where the ladies can slather their feet with soft and scented lotions, then slip on the cute cotton socks you've purchased at the dollar store. Buy an array of socks from bright solid colors to cute themed socks featuring bunnies and butterflies, and take fun and vibrant photos of everyone's sock-covered feet placed together.

This style of party is ideal for mornings or evenings, whenever there's a break in the wedding weekend event action, and even as the opening activities of your girls' sleepover or movie night.

Types of Treatments

Treat your party guests to a collection of unique spa treatments tailored to the season. In winter when dryness is a factor for most, have your spa menu feature moisturizing treatments. For instance, your spa experts could provide moisturizing facials and full-body exfoliating treatments in gentle exfoliant lotion form, not torturous scrubs performed in the shower. Hair experts can provide deep conditioning hair treatments and hot oil treatments to give hair extra shine for the next day. Skin specialists can apply deep conditioning creams to faces and elbows that will be exposed the next day.

Foot Treatments

Everyone's feet can use some TLC, so request the following gentle treatments, skipping anything grueling such as razoring dead skin from heels. In the wrong hands, those callus razors can take too much skin off, resulting in sore heels.

➤ Rose-scented foot soaks with rose petals in the water

➤ Relaxing lavender- and chamomile-scented foot soaks

➤ Aromatherapy foot messages with lotions scented with lavender, vanilla, invigorating lemon or tangerine, or exotic ginger and orange.

➤ Traditional pedicures with toenail painting

➤ Traditional pedicures with French pedicure nail polish

➤ Reflexology massage with the massage therapist hitting nerve points in the foot to relax you

Skin Treatments

➤ Full-body aromatherapy massage in light to medium pressure

➤ Exfoliating lotion application with a focus on elbows, knees, and other rough spots

Hair Treatments

➤ Deep conditioning treatments with jojoba oil

➤ Deep conditioning treatments specially formulated for ethnic hair

➤ Scalp massage with conditioning oils for hair

Brow Treatments

➤ Eyebrow shaping: tweezers

➤ Eyebrow shaping: threading

➤ Eyebrow makeup, including your cosmetics specialist providing each guest with the correct hue of eyebrow pencil to provide a natural eyebrow appearance, plus a lesson on proper brow filling

Watch Out!

What about facials? Beauty experts warn against getting a facial right before a wedding, since the chemicals used in traditional and specialty facials can cause redness and peeling— not a good look right before the wedding day. So leave this particular treatment off of your menu for any style of spa party and stick to less dangerous treatments such as massages and manicures.

Eyebrow waxing is a tad too dangerous on the day before the wedding, since a slip of the wax strip or an inexperienced specialist can tear half of your brow off or create a strange brow effect resulting in a true beauty disaster.

Massage

➤ Aromatherapy full body massage

➤ Cranial sacral massage (just head, jaw, and neck, a great stress releaser)

➤ Foot massage

➤ Hand massage

➤ Hot stone massage

➤ Island flower massage, using island flowers chosen for their healing and beautifying properties

Wraps

If you're at a salon, it's much easier to get a full body wrap with seaweed, detoxifying sea salt, or chocolate—applied and then showered off. It can be quite messy, so this one might best be left off your at-home party menu.

Watch Out!

It may be a fun trend for ladies' parties to offer a professional high-fashion makeup application, featuring dark makeup stripes and glue-on sparkles by the eyes, huge false eyelashes glued on, and other cosmetics effects, but no one should risk skin irritation, allergic reactions, or lasting marks from those glue-on effects the night before the wedding. Save this idea for an entirely different party.

Planning Details

With beauty at the center of your party's style, beauty will be a factor in all of your party preparations and will set the tone for your spa and pampering party. Think of the décor you see at an upscale spa; the clean, fresh, neutral tones; the soft earthy colors in sage green and sandy brows; the Zen feeling of the décor with lots of glass and stones and waterfalls. That very same mood-setting décor can be the guiding inspiration for your spa party elements.

Décor

Again, choose light hues in white and ivory, sea-glass blues and sage greens, especially tan colors. You and your party co-planners may have décor items in your homes that you can bring to your at-home party location to create a Zen, spalike atmosphere. For instance, if you have a portable waterfall, bring it to the party space and set it up at the entrance or in the massage room.

Green plants and especially bamboo plants are wonderful décor items for the natural feel of a spa party, so place those around the room. The craft store will be your mecca for easy, inexpensive décor items including $2 small round glass vases that you can fill with neutral-colored smooth river stones, and those become your table centerpieces set in a line, with each bowl six inches apart. Intersperse with scented votive candles in a coordinating shade of soft green or soft pink, and your party décor looks like it came right off of a magazine cover.

Sound is also part of your mood-setting décor, so play soft spalike music like wind flute or Native American music, soundscape soundtrack music like that of George Winston or R. Carlos Nakai. You'll find meditation music online that features the sounds of rainforests, also a wonderful soundtrack for your party's relaxing atmosphere.

Invitations

The soft neutral or spa-white color of your invitations show guests what they can expect to experience at this spa-themed party. The trend right now is to use color, rather than images, with solid-colored sand-beige being the number one choice in spa party color foundations. Lettering may be done in darker stone colors of brown, bamboo green, Caribbean blue, or the persimmon color of a dessert stony cliff.

If you do wish to use a spa image, you might choose a stylish illustration of a woman in a spa robe with her hair in a spa towel holding a bright orange drink or looking relaxed as she gets her nails done. Or, you might choose an image of a pastel-colored manicured hand holding a champagne glass.

I recently received a spa party invitation that was a sandy beige card with an illustration of a single white feather on it, and that conveyed perfectly the lightness of the party ahead.

A fun trend is including a spa-centric insert in printed and mailed invitations. One style-sharing and useful idea is printing up a list of aromatherapy scents paired with the effect they're said to convey and enclosing it with your invitation. Look at AuraCacia.com to find ready-made lists of aromatherapy scents and their benefits.

Menu Items

The menu at a spa party is comprised of so-called spa foods: gourmet bites made of healthy, fresh foods. No heavy, greasy or fried foods here. Consider these popular appetizers and platter foods served at today's spa-themed parties:

Steal My Party Idea

"We went to the craft store and bought a few bags of seashells, using those for our table centerpieces, placing a handful of shells in each little glass bowl."—Nancy, bridesmaid

Etiquette Friendly

Since teens and little girls are invited to spa parties as well, practice smart etiquette in the way you address the invitation by including the names of the ladies invited such as Janet Smith, Emily Smith and Ashley Smith, so the recipients know that young Emily and Ashley are invited to the party.

➤ Mango salsa on pita chips

➤ Endive topped with goat cheese

➤ Salmon mousse piped onto 3-inch lengths of fresh celery

➤ Mushroom caps stuffed with garlic cheese

➤ Shrimp cocktail

➤ Smoked salmon platter

➤ Fruit platters filled with exotic sliced fruits

➤ Veggie sushi in brown rice rolls

➤ California rolls

➤ Hummus dips and fresh veggies

At an upscale spa party, servers may walk around handing out hors d'oeuvres to your guests. At your home-based party, you may certainly place these fresh and healthy bites on a buffet table or place individual platters on different surfaces around your home. The dips and spreads may be on the kitchen island with pita breads and whole grain crackers surrounding them. The fresh seafoods and sushis may be on the dining room table. Wasabi pea snack mix may be on an end table. With all of your menu items arranged in matching white bowls, your menu takes on an upscale presentation style.

Drinks

Champagne and mimosas come to mind first for a spa party, but don't forget the refreshing taste of a green tea wine spritzer or sparkling fruit juices as your drink menu's creative themed choices. Sangrias are also popular at spa parties, as are large pitchers of water with cut fruits or veggies floating inside. One pitcher may bear cucumber water, and another may contain bright circles of lemons and limes. Set out footed water goblets for these spa-perfect drinks, and attach spa-themed wine charms to each glass so that guests can easily locate their own glasses during the party.

CHAPTER 22

Movie Nights

In This Chapter

➤ Selecting a movie

➤ Choosing your movie night atmosphere

➤ Preparing for your movie night

We've already touched on movie night as a possible theme for your families with kids group, and now we'll take another step into this wedding weekend event category. Specifically, we'll look beyond the kids' movie focus and look at airing the newest, hottest box office smash movies freshly out on DVD or on demand for an adult crowd. You invite the guests to your —or a friend's—decked-out home theater room or specious living room with its impressive big-screen HDTV, you cater for the party, and everyone grabs a space on your comfy couch, love seats, or pillowed floor seating gallery for a fabulous movie night at your place.

Hosts on a budget say this is one of the easiest and most enjoyable, no-pressure, no-investment parties to plan since they may already own a range of fantastic movies to show. And in this chapter, you're going to consider different types of movies, not just current blockbusters, to make a film festival in your own home.

Also in this chapter is the favorite activity of everyone going to the cineplex together, perhaps for the midnight showing of a top new movie release. Those guests with kids will love the return to how they used to see movies. "I can't even remember the last time I went to the movies after

Watch Out!

Don't invite disaster by e-mailing guests with an open question of what they want to see or you're going to get a diverse, endless list of movie titles, making your job of picking the biggest crowd-pleaser almost impossible. Always limit the voting list to a handful of movies.

2 pm," says Donald, groomsman and father of two . "So this late-night movie trip was a lot of fun for my wife and me."

A movie night party does offer the added perk of becoming a date night activity for guests.

Steal My Party Idea

"We planned for everyone to go to a midnight showing of Rocky Horror Picture Show. Our friends said they'd always wanted to go, so we dressed up in costume, brought our toast and other props, and joined in the interactive fun!"–Maura and Todd, newlyweds

Movie Choice

So how do you select the movie that will be shown at your movie night? A current trend is e-mailing guests with a please vote request, listing three or four current movies available on on demand or in your DVD collection. Everyone sends back their rankings of the movies, you tally the votes, and plan to show the winning movie.

Keeping the party to viewing one movie is usually the best option, since that's at least two hours of viewing timing, leaving an appropriate hour or two for mingling, enjoying your catering, and generally getting settled to watch the film. Asking guests to stay for two movies often extends the party past the point of comfort. If your party will include a trip to the multiplex, it's most realistic to choose one movie to see.

Of course, you're choosing from the current list of box office films for your trip to the cinema, and here are the most popular, crowd-pleasing categories that guests choose:

➤ Comedy

➤ Action-adventure

➤ Fantasy

Where's romantic comedy you might ask? Party hosts say that the rom-com is often a better choice when your movie night event is also a girls' night out. Yes, the men will attend when the movie is a romantic comedy starring Reese Witherspoon, Jennifer Aniston, or whomever the biggest rom-com star is at the time, but survey results say that mixed crowds prefer straight-up comedies and action films as their first choices.

Another category of film is the independent movie, for those who have a circle of guests who love their indie films and stars. When you plan a trip to a small art house theater to catch the newest Sundance hit, your movie night takes on an entirely different flavor, one that might match the personalities and preferences of your guests far better than the latest explosion-filled summer movie blockbuster.

Keep It Clean

Since you may have a mixed crowd of friends and those who are not well known to you, it's best to skip movies that have a lot of nudity, sex scenes, and controversial topics. Some people avoid that type of film as a rule, and it can be very awkward to sit in a room of people, including the bride's new in-laws, while a graphic sex scene is playing out on your big-screen TV.

What's Been Out For a While?

If you'll be going to a theater, new movie releases could present the challenge of packed attendance, and it can be tough to find rows of seats that allow everyone to sit together. So it might be a better choice to select a movie that's been out for a few weeks already, one that's not the top ticket draw at the movie theater. Even the biggest-name films stay in the theaters for weeks, so choosing one of those could make it a more comfortable viewing atmosphere. Your group might "own" the theater room.

What About Classic Films?

It's becoming a new trend to skip the current film releases and go to your collection of crowd-pleasing DVDs. At one recent movie night event, the host played *Some Like It Hot* for the Marilyn Monroe-loving couple and their friends who have never seen the genius of that film. Other classic films that are being chosen for movie night events include:

➤ *Breakfast at Tiffany's*

➤ *Singin' in the Rain*

➤ *Star Wars*

➤ Errol Flynn swashbuckling movies (compare these to the *Pirates of the Caribbean* films!)

➤ Classic horror films such as *Nosferatu*

➤ 80s classics such as *Sixteen Candles, Better Off Dead, The Breakfast Club*, and other quotable films.

A very fun trend for parties taking place during the weekends before the Christmas holidays is showing classic holiday movies. They might be

Money Mastery

Ask around to see who has the anniversary collectors' editions of classic films, so guests who have seen the movies before have some additional fascinating features to enjoy. If you have a Blu-ray player or 3D TV, be sure the DVD you borrow is compatible, and you're all set for free!

scheduled on a particular channel's Christmas movie marathon, on demand, or part of your personal movie DVD collection, but an invitation to view classic holiday stop-motion movies and sentimental classics like *It's a Wonderful Life* that people watch every year as a tradition—and paired with a winter treats food and drink menu—makes a winter wedding weekend an entirely enjoyable experience for all.

Setting Your Scene

Comfy seating is of the utmost importance, so much so that some party hosts move additional couches and bean bag chairs into the TV viewing room so that all guests have a roomy place to sit. Set up a buffet table to the side where your big boxes of pizza can be arranged, and place bowls of popcorn, snack mix, Junior Mints, and other bites on the coffee table, end tables, and other places within easy reach.

The best movie night atmosphere provides the ultimate in comfort, including a reclining chair or two, lots of elbow room, oversized bean bag chairs where a couple can cuddle, and even fluffy sleeping bags and pillows for little ones to rest (and perhaps fall asleep—if there are not too many explosions in the movie.)

If you have the budget, visit your local party supply rental agency to get a cart popcorn machine with a warm butter pump, as well as a retro ice cream bar freezer that guests will love. That's just the start of the foodie rental gear that can make your movie night unlike any other. Ask your rental agent what else you could rent: a hot dog cart, a cotton candy machine, a hot peanuts cart, and more.

Party-Planning Tips

A movie night offers such fun in the party details. You have your choice of theming the accents, invitations, and all else by the movie itself, such as a *Breakfast at Tiffany's* themed party with strings of pearls everywhere, and a stuffed cat. Or you could decorate your place to look like a movie theater.

Décor

To decorate your place like a movie theater, just hang movie posters everywhere. Ask friends and family members if they have any old movie posters—it doesn't have to be the poster of the movie you're screening! Any type of movie poster will do, inserted into an inexpensive metal-edged frame from the craft store, bought for even less with a coupon, for even less on a storewide sale day. Don't be picky about the movie title or stars for this décor-only piece, since this type of discount's trade-off is taking what you can get. If you do wish to hang themed posters, posters matching the movie you're showing, or movies starring a particular star, shop at Art.com for top-quality prints, or shop on eBay for stunningly inexpensive movie posters that may just come in prime condition.

Those cardboard cutouts of stars are a big hit for party décor, and you'll find them in mall stores and at mall kiosks, online at catalog websites, and through links found at a particular star's official fan sites. I've found fan sites to be extremely helpful, since a passionate fan is most likely to help others. I've been referred to reputable websites where I found a ton of exceptional décor items for a *Twilight*-themed party, including the very same life-size character window clings that Burger King used to decorate for its *Twilight* promotions, but now made it look as if Edward was standing outside the window, looking in at us. We uplit his figure outside too and it looked amazing. The price: under $15.

Money Mastery

Movie theaters, especially smaller independent ones, are one place to visit to ask for any leftover movie posters or cardboard cut-out displays that they have lying around, and the same goes for movie rental places like Blockbuster that have tons of movie posters and standup displays on hand. If you just ask, you will likely be able to take some for free.

In addition to movie posters and character cardboard cutouts for your theater-themed décor, see if you can borrow or rent a short length of velvet rope on those metal stands to place outside your front door. Not that guests have to wait to get in. It's just one of those fun décor touches, which often can be found at a rental agency or borrowed from a movie theater's supply of slightly damaged velvet rope stands in its back room (you may have to pay to borrow one of those—they're not cheap).

If you'll theme your party décor to fully match the movie you're showing, get creative with your decorations, using craft stores and especially party supply stores during the two months prior to and the weeks after the coordinating holiday or Halloween as your source of fabulous inexpensive theme-matching accents. For instance, your Oscars party at which you'll screen a top Oscar-contender movie could get you decorating with the little gold guy, whose likeness is on paper plates, tablecloths, and black napkins. You might be able to get a red carpet in a ten-foot length at a craft store, as well as cake stick-ins featuring big, dramatic silver and gold starbursts on wire, plus a chocolate Oscar for the top of the cake.

For an airing of a 1980s movie like *Sixteen Candles*, you might set out a pretty pink birthday cake—real, ready for slicing later on—backpacks and high school textbooks, Chinese food containers and chopsticks, and, of course, a pair of panties. Fans of the movie will appreciate the nuance. Humorous décor touches impress just as much as if you spent $300 to really deck the place out with pricy décor items.

Your themed plates, cups, and napkins become a focal point of any party, because that's what guests grab to help themselves to the food and drink. It's what they see closely, touch, balance on their laps, and have the closest experience with. So buy cute sets of theme-printed plates and service ware at a party supply store for this essential impression. As an added bonus to this style and its easy-breezy cleanup perks, are the number of eco-friendly party plates and service ware brands made from repurposed materials, so you don't have to worry about hurting the earth by purchasing disposable serving plates and cups, etc.

Money Mastery

Work your network to see who has a cloth-back director's chair you can borrow, who has a movie sound clapper, who has a pile of fun VHS tapes in their basement that you can borrow, dust off, and use as fun décor for your centerpiece or platforms for your buffet serving dishes to sit on. Just ask, and you shall receive lots of fun movie-themed items for your party's décor.

Invitations

Invitations and Evites can bear the images of a general movie night, either modern with neon light wording or retro with the dancing hotdog, popcorn cup, and soda container of 1950s and 1960s drive-in movie fame. Or, again, you can shop the theme décor aisles of party supply stores to find *Pirates of the Caribbean*, *Star Wars*, *Lord of the Rings*, and other movie collections. Displayed alongside the *Pirates* paper plates will be packets of invitations for you to fill out.

A quick Google search will deliver you to lots of free invitation templates created by DIY mavens, and I love what I'm seeing at Etsy.com with artists' creative invitations designed to suit a movie theme without using copyrighted images from the movie. It might be an elbow-length black glove to connote the *Breakfast at Tiffany's* theme or a dusty fedora to let guests know they're coming to an *Indiana Jones*—themed movie night. A plain white envelope with two red bite marks invites guests to watch *Twilight*, *New Moon*, or *Eclipse* on DVD, with guests invited to check off whether they're Team Edward or Team Jacob. With the head count for both, you can tailor your party favor goodie bags to include theme gifts for both camps.

Games

If the movie is the entertainment, are games needed? If your group is the type to love party games, plan a brief one, such as giving guests printed cards upon their arrival. On each card is ten or so challenging trivia questions about the movie you're all about to watch. Everyone takes the trivia quiz and drops their cards into a bowl or theme item like a fedora for the

Indiana Jones movie, and the winner is announced at the end of the movie viewing, with a great prize given to her. These types of movie trivia games played when a film is a classic that everyone has seen before, not when it's a current engrossing movie that demands silence and concentration, can have guests cheering and pointing out a trivia answer within the movie, making it an interactive game that keeps everyone's interest and energy levels high.

Menu

Take the expected movie menu and give it a twist. While you can and should serve traditional movie theater popcorn, set out some bowls of gourmet flavored popcorn such as white cheddar, jalapeno, and Cajun for an unexpected kick in a handful of movie popcorn.

I'm wild about kettlecorn's sweet and salty taste, so when I have a party, I look for cinnamon-flavored kettlecorn and other flavors such as these from KettleCornNYC.com:

➤ Chocolate: Sweet delicious cocoa glaze

➤ Caramel: Caramel glazed, sweeter than our most popular original flavor

➤ Cinnamon: Sweet and seriously cinnamon

➤ Regular: Movie theater-style salted popcorn/jumbo kernels

➤ Cheddar: Coated with a savory, real, all-natural white and yellow cheddar/not sweet

➤ Cheddar N'Spice: Infused with medium robust Cajun spices and coated with real, all-natural yellow cheddar

➤ Coconut: The sweet and savory coconut flavor is in the kernel, not candy coated

➤ Cotton Candy: Blue raspberry glaze, tastes like cotton candy

➤ Frutti Bam Bam: A trio of sweet and sour frutti, colorful glazes of cherry, grape and blue raspberry

➤ Chocolate N'Caramel: Rich blend of chocolate and caramel glazed

➤ Sour Cream N'Chives: Speaks for itself, savory, not sweet

➤ Spicy Cajun BBQ: Infused with medium robust Cajun spices

➤ Spicy Ranch: Infused with medium robust Cajun spices and coated with a savory ranch

➤ Chili Lime: Infused with medium robust chili spices

Serve popcorn in paper cones that you make as the simplest ever DIY project. Kids can help decorate the paper or wax paper cones they've curled and stapled to make, and guests use these cones to help themselves to your popcorn or snack mixes. Plastic dessert bowls too make great easy help-yourself or share-it servings of snacks.

Popcorn aside, regular-sized boxes of M&Ms, Junior Mints, Twizzlers and other concession stand candies let adult and child guests indulge in movie theater sweets, as do fresh-baked bready pretzels in full twisted size or those little pretzel fingers that movie theaters offer. Again, twist this with a sprinkling of sea salt on the pretzel, and give guests their choice of cheesy dipping sauces, from traditional cheddar to white cheddar to ranch dressing to spicy garlic mustard.

A hot dog bar allows your guests to fix their own dogs with such toppings as sauerkraut, chili, cheese, diced green peppers, relish, and more. And, of course, a fries bar filled with regular fries, sweet potato fries, Tater Tots, waffle fries, and different flavorings such as Cajun and Old Bay—served in those paper cones and with dipping sauces like ketchup, mayo, garlic mustard, and tartar sauce give your fries bar a special kick.

Drinks

Beverages can run the range from bottle-poured sodas to gourmet-flavored soda like pomegranate fizz and Meyer lemon, to beers and mixed drinks, wines and sangrias.

Favors

Send guests home with boxes of candies or chocolate bars, the same types you'd find in a movie theater concessions stand. A new trend for small groups is giving out gift cards for movie rentals or movie night theme gift sets such as six square popcorn serving cups packaged together found in such stores as Bed Bath & Beyond.

Favors matched to current and classic movie themes still provide you with great goodie bag items:

➤ Baggies of snack treats

➤ Keychains with a character on them

➤ Movie-themed collectors' cards

➤ Temporary tattoos with the movie's logo or a word or phrase from the movie

➤ Movie-themed notepads or Post-It® notes from the dollar store

- ➤ Movie-themed candies, packaged in special movie logo wrappers
- ➤ Tiny gift books of movie trivia, or a small square of paper on which you've printed one or more movie trivia questions
- ➤ Movie- or character-themed bookmarks such as ones that picture Marilyn Monroe, James Dean, *Star Wars*, *The Godfather*, *Twilight*, and *Harry Potter*, found at bookstores.
- ➤ Theme-shaped chocolates found at local chocolate stores and paired to the movie's theme.

CHAPTER 23

After the Wedding Weekend

In This Chapter

➤ Expressing thanks

➤ Sharing photos

➤ Cleanups and fixes

After all the fun has been had during your wedding weekend, a few essential things need to be arranged. And if you're the bride, several of them need to be arranged before you go on your honeymoon. In this chapter, you'll learn how to organize your post-wedding closing tasks, including sending thank-you notes and gifts to those who organized and perhaps paid for several fun wedding weekend events, sharing fabulous photos of guests enjoying the get-togethers, and—most importantly—being gracious and arranging for professional cleanings (and perhaps repairs) of the hosts' homes and other properties.

Some of these tasks can be left until after your honeymoon, and some—such as professional cleanings—need to be arranged before you leave. This section will help you schedule these all-important To-Dos and cement your status as a dream bride and groom who have every thoughtful detail covered.

Saying Thank-You to Hosts

No matter the style, size, theme, location, or budget of the wedding weekend event that a loved one hosted for you, it's an essential etiquette task for you to send the host or hosts a hand-written thank-you note, and many brides and grooms also choose to send those hosts a wonderful thank-you gift to accompany it. After all, party and outing hosts have invested lots of their precious personal time, and often a nice chunk of money, in planning an exciting, enjoyable event that added to the unforgettable nature of your entire wedding weekend.

Thanks to them, your friends and family had so much more to look forward to during their trip to your wedding town. Long-distance friends were able to mingle and meet each others' babies and kids. Family members were able to spend more time together than the wedding itself would have allowed. And you got to unwind, laugh, and also get more valuable time to spend with your long-distance friends and family. That's quite a gift the hosts gave to you all!

Speaking of gifts, it's quite common for a wedding weekend event to be the hosts' actual wedding gift to you, a priceless present of an experience rather than a wrapped gift off of your registry. If a relative or friend has given you an event as your present, it's wise to send a heartfelt thank you to the hosts right away, as soon as possible, not to wait those weeks or months for your thank-you portraits and cards to come in. I strongly advise that you send the event hosts an impressive personalized thank-you card and gift right away.

Thank-You Notes

In wedding world, a swirl of etiquette rules surround thank-you notes. For this particular thank-you, you have just a few to keep in mind. The first is that your thank-you note should be written and delivered immediately. Many brides and grooms pop theirs in the mail the day before the wedding so it reaches the hosts just a day or two after the event they hosted. Some couples write out a stack of thank-yous before their wedding day and ask a parent to pop them in the mail a day or two after the wedding so they're received shortly afterward. Your close friends and family members who hosted your wedding weekend party will be thrilled and impressed that you took the time to write out your expression of thanks, that it mattered so much to you when you had so much else going on.

If you cannot get these thank-you notes out before you return from your honeymoon, that's okay as well. Some couples prefer to personalize these thank-yous with photos taken at the event or with a gift that they bought for the event hosts while on their honeymoon.

The second etiquette rule to obey is that this thank-you note, like your wedding gift thank-you notes, needs to be written out by hand—not e-mailed or texted, and not simply with your names signed on the bottom of a preprinted thank-you stationery card.

Here are some examples of how you might word your thank-you notes:

➤ Dear Aunt Mary and Uncle John: Thank you so much for everything you did to create such a wonderful cocktail party during our wedding weekend. Everything was beautiful, and we're still talking about that amazing rum drink! It meant the world to us to spend time with you and with the other guests as our wedding weekend began, and we love you very much for giving us such an unforgettable party!

➤ Dear Lisa and Tim: Everyone had a blast at the pool party! We can't thank you enough for opening up your home (and your hot tub!) to us and to our friends and family. It was a fantastic highlight of our wedding weekend, and everyone said they felt like they were at a five-star resort! From the toast to the dinner and the hours sitting by your fire pit, it was the perfect evening, thanks to your amazing hospitality and generosity.

➤ Dear Mom and Dad: Thank you so much for everything you did to help us create our dream wedding weekend! Everything you planned came out beautifully, and the morning-after breakfast was perfection! We feel so lucky and so blessed to have such wonderful parents! Thank you.

As mentioned, you might wish to enclose in your thank-you note a photo, or several photos, from the event itself, as a way of sharing your favorite memories from the event planned in your honor.

Thank-You Gifts

Again, no matter the size, scope, and expense of the event thrown for you, it's a wonderful idea to thank the hosts with a thoughtful gift. Here are some top thank you gift choices to consider:

➤ A bottle of champagne or wine

➤ A generous box of Godiva chocolates

➤ A lush floral arrangement in a gorgeous vase delivered to their home

➤ A basket of gourmet goodies, such as baked treats, teas or coffees, and tea breads. If a friend hosted a movie night, for instance, it can be in keeping with the party theme to send a tin of flavored popcorn.

Steal My Party Idea

"Before and during the party, I made sure that we took lots of gorgeous photos of my friend's house and backyard party areas, which looked amazing with tons of lit candles, floral arrangements, the buffet, and more. I wanted to capture how beautiful their home looked, and create an amazing collection of photos that we would then give to them after the wedding weekend to show them how much we appreciated every detail they put into decorating for the party. We created an inexpensive photo book with those photos, with our messages about what we loved—the caviar, the champagne, the gardenias— printed on each page with each photo as a visual thank-you note."—Lila, bride

➤ A gift card to a local fine restaurant for the hosts' own date night

Whatever you decide to give to the hosts, be sure to put extra effort, care, and creativity into wrapping the gift beautifully, not just plop it into a gift bag from the card store. Every minute detail of this gift should show that you took the time to design something very special.

Sharing Photos and Video

After the party, sporting event, picnic, that adventurous ride to a waterfall, or any type of wedding weekend event, be sure to post your best digital photos to a photo-sharing site such as Kodak Gallery or Shutterfly, and then e-mail those who hosted and attended the event with an invitation to view your collection of shots. Since a wedding weekend is all about togetherness and spending quality time with people you don't get to see very often, those group photos and duo snapshots become very valuable to all. Your friends and family will certainly wish to order photos from your amazing wedding weekend events, and when you post to an easy-share site, they can do so using their own existing accounts (and credit cards). You won't need to take orders for people. It's all up to them to place their own.

Etiquette Friendly

It's okay to share an amazing sight from your destination wedding with those you could not invite. Those who love you will enjoy getting a look at your celebration's special moments and will appreciate your thinking of them.

For momentous occasions, such as running into a celebrity while touring a metropolitan area, chancing upon a scene of dolphins swimming past your beachfront party, kids doing adorable things, and more, post your own digital video to YouTube, and share the link with family and friends who would love to see your footage. If your wedding was a destination wedding and the weekend events were enjoyed by your small handful of destination wedding guests, these video snippets may be viewed by your larger circle of friends and family upon your e-mailed notification.

Cleanups and Fixes to Party Locales

When a wedding weekend event takes place in someone's home or vacation home, it's a classy, gracious move to offer professional cleaning both before and after the celebration. But be sure to ask if the hosts want that type of service, since some people aren't comfortable having cleaning crews in their home or accepting such a generous offer from you when it was their offer to host the party.

Many home party hosts do appreciate the offer for professional cleaning after the party, looking forward to spot removal from their carpets, rug shampooing, and a thorough return to their preparty orderly environment. If the hosts wish to take you up on your offer, talk with them to decide which of you will select the cleaning agency, and the best manner of scheduling service. The hosts will likely prefer to speak to the company themselves and set up their own appointment.

If, by chance, anything in the home was stained, marred, broken, or otherwise damaged, it's up to you to pay for the repairs. This may include tablecloths stained with food, broken glasses or dishes, hopefully something small and easily repaired rather than a shattered sliding glass door, ruined hardwood floor, or other disastrous damage to a home. To protect yourself in case of larger damage and expensive repairs, talk with the homeowner about the big trend of house party hosts getting extra insurance coverage specifically for a special event held in their home. Their insurance company likely offers these types of riders, covering them and you in case of any disasters. These days, with repairs so expensive and houseguests (unfortunately) so ready to sue if they eat a bad clam or get into a car accident on the way home, it would be quite a gamble to skip home event insurance. And, of course, offer to pay for the rider as a matter of good etiquette and decency. It's not as expensive as you might think.

Repairs to Vehicles

If anyone who drove your guests to events suffers any scratches to the exterior or stains from spills on the interior, offer to cover expenses for their repairs. You can do that interior stain removal work yourself, or you can offer to take the car to a car wash for professionals to work out those smudges and smears for an affordable price.

Damages at an Establishment

Let's say your party was held at a restaurant, and during the course of the event a guest of yours caused damage to their property. While most restaurants, museums, and other establishments do have insurance of their own, be aware that there may be a line in the contract you signed stating that any damages caused at your event are your responsibility to repair. Many brides and grooms wonder about the diplomacy of this dilemma: do you just pay for it yourself, or do you charge the guest?

Watch Out!

Before you forward the establishment's bill for repairs to the offender who caused the damage in question, be sure to blacken out your personal information such as credit card numbers and the like. The offender will not be happy to receive this bill, and you certainly don't want the rude guest (or the drunk, sloppy date of a friend who caused the problem) to victimize you with identity theft. This, sadly, has happened, and I don't want it happening to you.

If the damage was caused by an accident, most brides and grooms do pay for the fix. If the guest was misbehaving, drunk, aggressive, or destructive, you're within your rights to submit a bill for the repairs to them with a straightforward, detailed request to pay for the damage they caused to the window/door/table, whatever may have taken the impact. Yes, this is uncomfortable to do, and the rude guest may refuse to pay, but you must take proper, self-respecting steps to remedy the situation. If the guest doesn't pay, you will have to cover the costs yourself. You don't want the establishment to take you to court for nonpayment of repairs. With the contract on their side, you'll have no chance of avoiding the responsibility, and you'll waste extra money on court fees.

WORKSHEETS

Use the following worksheets to keep yourself ultra-organized as you plan your wedding weekend event.

As you know, being organized cuts down on planning stress and can save you money. Keeping track of what you're buying, when, and for how much helps you avoid extra spending in any category.

So use these worksheets for the fastest, easiest, and most efficient way to keep all of your info in one place. With your party plans made efficient and organized, you'll have much more fun putting together a fabulous event the bride and groom and all of the guests will love.

Event Details

Event Type	Event Location	Event Date	Event Time

Guest List

Name	E-mail	RSVP Received √	Attending √

Shopping Lists

Item	Type/Style/Color	How Many Needed	Where to Buy	Who's Buying

Budget Chart

Item	$ Budgeted	Actual Cost	Paid √
Invitations			
Catering			
Cake			
Desserts			
Drinks: alcohol			
Drinks: mixers			
Ice			
Rental items			
Décor			
Craft items			
Entertainment			
Experts (spa and beauty, massage, etc.)			
Transportation			
Games			
Favors			
Photography and video			
Other:			

RESOURCES

The following websites are listed here for your research purposes. We don't endorse any particular sites, and we encourage you to practice smart online shopping at all times!

Invitations:

Evite.com
Hallmark.com
Mountaincow.com
Papyrusonline.com
Pingg.com
PSAEssentials.com
Shindigz.com
Shutterfly.com
WeddingMapper.com

Crafts and DIY Items:

BellaCupcakeCouture.com (cupcake wrappers!)
Kmart.com
Michaels.com
Target.com
Walmart.com
Wilton.com (cake and cupcakes supplies)

Coupons and Deals:

CouponCabin.com
CouponMountain.com
Coupons.com
RetailMeNot.com
SwagGrabber.com

Favors and Gifts:

Amazon.com
AuraCacia.com
Bn.com (Barnes and Noble)
BathandBodyWorks.com

CafePress.com
CherylandCompany.com
CustomInk.com
eBay.com
Envirosax.com
Godiva.com
KateAspen.com
Kodak.com
Shutterfly.com
Target.com
Tiffany.com
Walmart.com

Food and Cakes:

AllRecipes.com
Bethenny.com
BHG.com (Better Homes and Gardens)
CookingLight.com
Costco.com
FoodandWine.com
FoodNetwork.com
HansenCakes.com
Kings.com
MarthaStewart.com
MixingBowl.com
PaulaDeen.com
RachaelRayMag.com
SamsClub.com
Wilton.com
WholeFoods.com

Drinks:

Bethenny.com
Cocktail.com
Cocktails.About.com
CocktailTimes.com
DrinkJockey.com
DrinkMixer.com
Evite.com (bar stock calculator!)
FoodNetwork.com

SuperCocktails.com
ThatstheSpirit.com
TheBar.com
Webtender.com
WineSpectator.com

Restaurants:

Restaurants.com
travelandleisure.com
Yelp.com
Zagats.com

Travel:

AAA.com
BnBFinder.com
Expedia.com
Festivals.com
OnLocationVacations.com
Orbitz.com
ParkInfo2Go.com
ResortsOnline.com
Towd.com (Tourism Office Worldwide Directory)

Check the websites for the hotel chains you're considering—they often have group rates for special events like weddings and family reunions!

THE AUTHOR

Sharon Naylor is the author of over 35 wedding-planning books, including *The Ultimate Bridal Shower Idea Book* and other titles for the bridesmaid and maid of honor. She is the Bridesmaid specialist for BridalGuide.com, a wedding Q&A expert for iVillage Weddings, a contributor to *Southern Bride*, host of 'Here Come the Moms' on Wedding Podcast Network, contributor to the top bridal magazines, and a featured guest expert on such shows as Good Morning America, ABC News, Get Married, I Do! with The Knot, Lifetime, and many more.

Publisher's Weekly recently named three of her newest wedding books as among the best wedding titles of the year, and her books on bridal showers, etiquette, budget planning, personalizing your wedding, bridesmaid advice, and tips for the moms have all sat at the #1 spot on Amazon.com's best-sellers in wedding books and Kindle downloads.

In recent news, she is the Wedding Advice Guru for Weddzilla.com, a wedding Q&A expert for WeddingMapper.com, and a contributor to many award-winning bridal blogs.

Sharon's bridal and travel articles have been syndicated by Creators Syndicate, appearing in thousands of media outlets across the country and the world, and her video segments are in-demand by Fortune 500 companies and wedding industry entrepreneurs.

She has been featured in *InStyle Weddings, Modern Bride, Brides, Bridal Guide, Glamour, Marie Claire, Self, Shape, Redbook, The Wall Street Journal* and many other top publications. Visit her website www.sharonnaylor.net for more on her books and to access her free worksheet downloads.

INDEX

Y

Z